W9-AOJ-406

ST. CHARLES COUNTY COMMUNITY COLLEGE

RASPUTIN
RASCAL MASTER

JANE OAKLEY

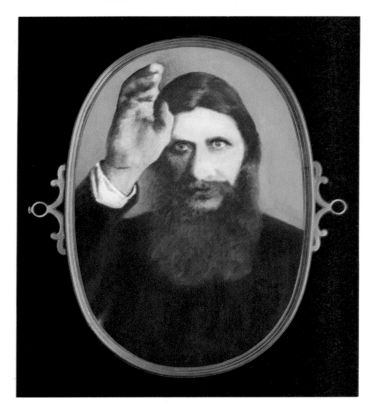

St. Martin's Press • New York

RASPUTIN – Rascal Master
was produced by
Labyrinth Publishing S.A. Switzerland

Design by Sandipa Gould Griffin
Front cover design by Doris Borowsky

Copyright © 1989 by Jane Oakley

All rights reserved. Printed in Spain.
No part of this book may be used or reproduced in any manner
without written permission except in the case of brief quotations
embodied in critical articles or reviews. For information, address
St. Martin's Press, 175 Fifth Avenue, New York, NY 10010

Printed by Cronion S.A. Barcelona, Spain

Typeset on Apple Macintosh by Ma Premo (S. Castelli)
at Microprint – Via Pacini 49 / 51, Florence, Italy

Library of Congress Cataloging in Publication Data

Oakley, Jane
      Rasputin / Jane Oakley
            p.   cm.
      ISBN 0 - 312 - 03227 - 7
      1. Rasputin, Grigori Efimovich, ca. 1870 – 1916.
      2. Soviet Union -- Court and courtiers -- Biography.
      3. Soviet Union -- History -- Nicholas II, 1894 – 1917.
      I. Title
      [DK 254 · R3025   1990]
      947 -- dc 20
                                                        89 - 77076
                                                        CIP

First Edition
10 9 8 7 6 5 4 3 2 1

Contents

Rasputin: Man, Mystic, Messiah, Myth

Rasputin's life was a powerful mixture of bizarre fictions and even more remarkable fact. The legend reached mythological proportions in his own lifetime and in the seventy years since his death, Rasputin has joined Cesare Borgia, Genghis Khan, and Caligula, amongst others, in the pantheon of Satanic supermen. The name Rasputin is recognized universally with a frisson of excitement and recoil; "The Mad Monk" and "Russia's Greatest Love Machine" are just two of the sobriquets of the man who, single-handed, it was claimed, brought down the Romanov dynasty in an orgy of sex and intrigue and dark satanic practices.

In fact, Rasputin's life did consist of most of the ingredients necessary to make a popular archfiend: the humblest of origins; intimations of supernatural power; erotomania; religious fervor; intimacy and undue influence with the Russian royal family; and an outlandish and mesmerizing appearance. Although he was to become synonymous in the popular imagination with wickedness and wild sexual and sorcerous excess, if the lurid overlay is taken away the man that remained was larger than life and even more surprising.

But the nature of Russia also played its part in the legend. Vast and unfathomable, it sprawls over more than a sixth of the world's surface, extending from the Arctic to the Pacific Oceans, from the Baltic to the Black Seas. In Europe and yet not of it, Russia is a continent of its own. Mysterious, inscrutable and tragic on a grand scale, it owes virtually

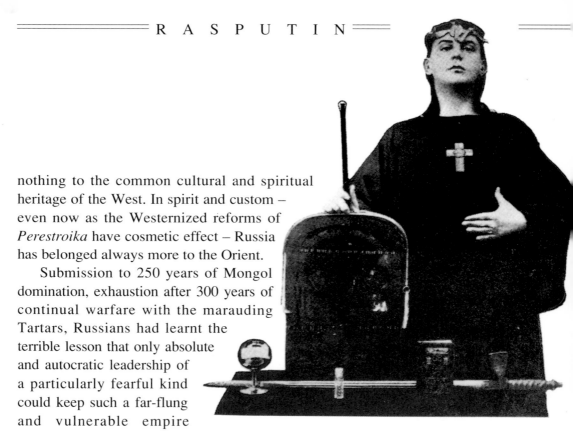

nothing to the common cultural and spiritual heritage of the West. In spirit and custom – even now as the Westernized reforms of *Perestroika* have cosmetic effect – Russia has belonged always more to the Orient.

Submission to 250 years of Mongol domination, exhaustion after 300 years of continual warfare with the marauding Tartars, Russians had learnt the terrible lesson that only absolute and autocratic leadership of a particularly fearful kind could keep such a far-flung and vulnerable empire together. Only absolute power over the people could ensure the almost super-human efforts to defend continually almost infinite boundaries with few natural frontiers. And so they submitted to the often flamboyant and awesomely brutal rule of their Tsars, and they turned to religion, superstition and a mystical fatalism to get them through their most miserable times.

The Tsar of all the Russias, Nicholas II, who was to let Rasputin into the heart of this absolute power, was a kindly, sensitive, family-minded man, ill-equipped to shoulder the enormous burden of state, and temperamentally ill-suited to the necessarily ruthless and decisive execution of that power. His character was far removed from the epic blood-thirstiness which had made so many of his predecessor's reigns so memorable. His energies were naturally turned inwards to the welfare of his family and court rather than to the seething and increasingly dissatisfied mass of his people from whom he grew increasingly remote.

Rasputin appeared to come as an envoy from one of the most remote regions of the Tsar's empire. He was a man of exceptional energy and power who retained the simplicity and strength of the Siberian peasant. He appeared to the isolated monarch to be a link with the true spirit of Russia and with the religious power of her past. Above all, Rasputin came as a God-sent healer for the one person who mattered most to Nicholas ll and his wife Alexandra – the Tsarevitch Alexis, his only heir, their beloved hemophiliac son.

Rasputin remained this Siberian peasant as he moved through every stratum of Russian society. He brought his rude clothes, his rough manners, his heavily-accented, straightforward mode of speech into the Imperial palaces, right into the boudoirs of the Tsar and Tsaritsa and their family. He was a blast of cold air from the steppes through a Court that was corrupt, full of self-interest, bloated with self-indulgence and riven with factions.

Rasputin swaggered across the vast stage of Russian life at the beginning of the 20th century, playing to the full all the four roles destiny had handed him – Man, Mystic, Messiah and Myth.

And so the story starts with the child who was father to the man.

Part I

RASPUTIN:
THE MAN

Siberia
The Wild

*Rasputin's house
in Pokrovskoe –
a humble, simple
and well-kept
home in a
Siberian village.*

Rasputin's own family history, memorialized by his daughter Maria, relates how a great meteor flamed across the skies of western Siberia on the night of 23rd January, 1871. Sight of such a shooting star was recognized by the superstitious peasants as a sign of some significant or momentous event. In the village of Pokrovskoe, which lay in that meteor's arcing track, a baby was born that night. He was to be baptized Grigori Efimovich Rasputin. But the villagers of Pokrovskoe, and the rest of Russia, were to have to wait another three decades before they were to understand the significance of that celestial sign.

The village of Pokrovskoe is in Western Siberia, some 200 miles east of the Ural Mountains and about 1600 miles from St. Petersburg. The traveling time from the capital to Rasputin's own village would then have been anything between six and eight days, by railway, river and road. It was a sizable and relatively prosperous village in Rasputin's time. Commercially and strategically it was important being a river stop on the River Tura, part of the extensive and much used Ob system of rivers which flowed from the source in China to its final outlet in the Arctic Ocean. In the summer, when the river was broad and

11

Changing horses in a Siberian village – a harsh environment meant tough conditions for the people and animals. The main form of transport was horses pulling sleighs which moved across the iced rivers, to deliver post and goods.

fast flowing, steamships would ply between the provincial capital at Tobolsk, 120 miles to the north, and the nearest town to Pokrovskoe, Tyumen, about 60 miles to the west. In winter, when the great rivers were frozen solid, the passengers and goods would be loaded onto carts and sledges to make the rougher ride across the ice and down the muddied, potholed roads. Rasputin's village was a staging post where horses would be changed on the grueling trans-Siberian crossings. This part of Siberia is flat with a vast, almost limitless horizon. Marshy in spring and early summer, then parched by the sun, and blanketed in snow and ice for almost half a year, the climate was extreme and inhospitable. Scattered through the marshland on slightly higher ground were tracts of dark, forbidding, evergreen trees. It was a harsh environment which produced a tough, hardy people who relieved the hardships of everyday life with uproarious drinking bouts, and energetic singing and dancing.

The Siberian Peasant

Rasputin was born the second son of a well-to-do peasant farmer who owned enough horses to supply fresh stock to the sledges, carts and carriages which used his village as a staging-post. The Siberian peasant differed from the Russian peasant in that he had never been subject to the serfdom which crushed the Russian, and in effect was far more extensive and in some ways even more vicious, than the slavery in the southern states of America. In Russia in the middle of the 18th century a Russian serf, in fact a slave, owned by a nobleman, was denied every right; to dispose of his life and labor where he chose, to live with his family, to work for his own livelihood, to own land, to call upon the law for protection. Not only was he denied his liberty, he could not even claim the right to life.

The historian Tibor Szamuely points out that there is barely any history of the lives of these slaves; that even great Russian writers and historians have been reluctant to face squarely the full extent of this denial of the basic human rights of an oppressed class which numbered, at times, up to 90% of the Russian population. Writing of the middle of the 18th century he

Almost akin to the wild west of America, the tough life was managed by wild people, who supplemented their harsh environment with heavy bouts of drinking, between long hours of work and the hardship of everyday life.

characterized one element of this bondage; "Every year hundreds and thousands of slaves were murdered by their masters, yet only in a very few cases of extreme cruelty on a mass scale were the perpetrators, upon the personal intervention of the monarch [there was no protection in law] brought to book and condemned...to do penance in church for their sins." Only in 1861 was serfdom abolished by the Tsar Alexander II, but the harsh legacies of absolute oppression, submission and impotence in the face of authority, was deeply etched into the Russian psyche.

For a peasant, until the end of the 19th century, Siberia was a preferable place to live. It was the Wild West of Russia. And like the Wild West it encouraged an independent, pioneering spirit. Vast, inhospitable, ill-served by road and rail, sparsely populated, used as a place of exile for criminals and unfortunates who had displeased their masters, Siberia, nevertheless, was free. These features made it distinctly unappealing to the aristocracy and meant therefore that there had been very few masters to command whole armies of serfs; that no tradition of serfdom had left its stain on the Siberian soul.

So Rasputin was born to a hard, rough life but with no cultural legacy of oppression. He had only the authority of his hard-working, heavy-drinking father over him and only the basic laws of his village with which to comply.

The people were strongly individual, never slaves, always retaining their own personal strength and independence – like pioneers all over the world, they formed the uniqueness of their own country.

Vodka was a central feature of peasant life, the source of warmth, celebration and comradeship.

Not only did the Siberian peasant have a chance of owning and cultivating his own land, of building his own business, of plying his own trade; his freedom from slavery meant that his spirit was independent, optimistic and proud. He looked only to God and to the Tsar, his "Little Father", as having dominion over him. Other Russians looked on the Siberian as narrow, isolated, hopelessly out of touch and uninterested in anything which went on west of the Urals. In many ways this was true. His faith was deeply held but often less than orthodoxly practiced; there was room for widespread superstition and some distinctly unorthodox religious sects. Folk tales, folk medicine, folk magic, all added to the richness and primitive vigor of the Siberian experience. Singing and dancing was also an enjoyable outlet for their robust, instinctive natures.

Drink too, specifically vodka, was a central feature of peasant life. So much was drunkenness a way of life that even in law you were not considered liable for your actions if it could be proved that you were drunk at the time. Sober, a man could get up to two years penal labor for assaulting a minor official: if drunk, he could be imprisoned for a mere three days for beating up even the judge. This endemic alcoholism meant that village life was characterized, particularly on feast days and holidays, by brawling, abuse, and easy promiscuity. It was a harsh and, at times, brutal environment.

"Whoever has looked at beauty is marked out already by death."

A contemporary witness of a Siberian holiday described vividly the abandonment of even the womenfolk to drink and tomfoolery; "I saw a whole crowd of women singing and dancing, some of them had red ribbons pinned to their headscarves, some wore their sheep-skin coats inside out, others wore comic headgear and hats: they carried sticks and wreaths of flowers, one of them had a bale of straw. As they came to the side streets they would set a bale of straw alight, jump over it, stamp out the fire and go on their way. They threw snow at any man they encountered and tried to knock him to the ground; they were all perfectly drunk, stumbling into one another, falling over, four or five at a time, slipping over together shrieking on the ice, throwing up their legs and revealing the most remarkable sights. Their songs made use of words that are not to be found in any dictionary...The following day, and a terrible snowstorm notwithstanding, crowds of drunken and frenzied women were still staggering about the village." And that was just the women.

But along with this coarseness and lack of refinement came a warmth and generosity of spirit. No stranger, whether wandering holy man or criminal on the run, was turned away without food and often shelter. Maria Rasputin remembered how seldom the family would sit down to a meal alone; there was always somebody who needed a meal. There was even a custom of leaving a bowl of bread and milk outside the door at night in case any passing stranger was hungry.

The Making of the Man

Grigori Rasputin had the normal childhood of a boy growing up in a village in Siberia at the end of the 19th century. He had barely any formal education, until he learnt the rudiments from the monks he met when a grown man. His daughter recalled, however, that her father had a remarkable memory and could remember whole passages of the Bible after just one reading. At about the age of ten he began to work on the land full time, alongside his father and elder brother. From quite early it was evident that this second son of Efim and Anna Rasputin was no ordinary boy. His daughter Maria described the stories her grandparents told her about the childhood of her extraordinary father.

As a child he showed an uncanny ability to calm and even heal the farm animals. One such story concerned one of the family's horses which, as they all sat down for the family meal, their father mentioned had gone lame. Without a word, Rasputin got up from the table and went to the stable and there, watched in puzzlement by his father, he went unhesitatingly to the horse's lame leg and placed his hand on the offending tendon. He stood for a while, his eyes closed, his head tilted back, in apparently deep concentration.

*Siberian
village elders
pose before a
water cart.*

Then, rousing himself, he patted the horse and was heard to say "You're all better". Rasputin's father was an uneducated and unimaginative man and he could never understand or approve of this dreamy, other-worldly side of his son. Nevertheless, he was intrigued to see what, if any, effect this had had on his horse. He led it into the yard and was amazed to see no sign of a limp or other discomfort. But unexplained phenomena alarmed him and more often than not he was to think it the work of the devil. For this reason, he did not appreciate being told by his son when an old friend of his, a horse trader, was lying and selling him a horse whose provenance was far inferior to what was claimed. All through his life Rasputin was to have a marked ability for reading men's real motives, for judging character and seeing the essential man behind the mask.

As a child, he discovered what seemed to be an extraordinary gift of second-sight. But as Rasputin explained to his daughter, in childhood he had thought that everyone could see what he did, that his ability was not out of the ordinary at all:

> *"I used to play with the children of Pokrovskoe and quarreled
> with them, but I never dared to steal or pilfer the smallest thing.
> I used to believe that everybody would at once see that I had
> stolen something since I, myself, was aware of it as soon as one
> of my comrades had stolen. Even when he had stolen in a dis-
> tant place and hidden the object he had taken, I could always
> see the object behind him."*

took place in Rasputin's father's house – discussions about problems such as the loss of a horse, in this case stolen by one of the men at the meeting, recognized by the child Rasputin.

Another story went that, while still a boy, Grigori Rasputin was lying in his house by the fire, with the fever which had kept him indoors for the past few days. His father was by then headman of the village. A number of men from their village had come round to see him about the theft of a horse. (Horse thieving was one of the most common activities of the Siberian peasant.) There was a great deal of talk backwards and forwards about who could have taken this horse; the most obvious explanation seemed to be that one of the numerous brodyagi, who passed through the village on their wanderings, must have seen his opportunity and made off with the beast. Suddenly the young Rasputin arose from his sick-bed and, pointing a finger at one of the richest and most respected villagers, declared that it was he who had stolen the horse. There was uproar. The man denied it furiously; Rasputin's father was angered and embarrassed and if his son had not been unwell he would have beaten him then and there for his presumption.

However, some of the men at that meeting could not dismiss so easily the remarkable authority with which this child had spoken. That night they decided to follow the man Rasputin had accused, back to his smallholding. There, as they watched in the shadows, they saw him slip into his yard and lead out the very horse that had been stolen.

It was the custom to execute a summary justice, which given the brutish nature of these hard men living in a harsh land, meant a severe beating to within a few inches of the miscreant's life. The thief was duly left unconscious and bleeding in the snow. The horse was returned to its owner and the story of the young lad Rasputin's uncanny ability to recognize the thief, despite the fact that he had been in bed with a fever when the horse had been stolen and so could not have witnessed the event, began to circulate the village. These tricks, however, did not impress his father. He often lost his temper with his obstinate son who would rather daydream than work, and he had no compunction in beating him for what he saw as laziness, as he himself had been beaten by his father in a custom which raised few eyebrows in that simple society.

At age 12, Rasputin saw his elder brother Mikhail drowned in the local river – an event that changed his whole life.

As Grisha the boy began to enter adulthood and become Grigori Rasputin the man, he had to take his place in a community of which he never felt entirely a part, and conflicts and ostracism were inevitable.

When Rasputin was about twelve years old a tragedy happened that changed his whole attitude to life, and even more profoundly – so his sister claimed – his temperament and abilities. He and his older brother Mikhail, or Misha as he was known in the family, would often swim and fish in the River Tura that ran beside their village and was so vital a part in the trade and prosperity of everyone's lives there. One hot day, probably in the summer of 1883, the two brothers went swimming, but not in their usual spot. Misha was the first to jump into the swift flowing stream but to Rasputin's horror he saw Misha attempt to stand up, but miss his footing and disappear beneath the water. Rasputin rushed to the river bank, crying for his brother, and thrust his arm into the water where he had last seen Misha. In his panic, Misha grasped this proffered hand so forcefully that Rasputin also tumbled into the swirling waters.

The two boys were washed downstream as they clung together, attempting to regain some footing. At last a local farmer hearing their cries ran to the bank and managed to fish them both out. They were taken home, both half-drowned and both developed what was diagnosed then as an inflammation of the chest, which was most probably pneumonia. The nearest doctor was about 60 miles away at Tyumen. But there was little that medicine could have done

When Rasputin was a grown man with children of his
own he took his young children for a walk in the woods
near his home and showed them the very spot where some
sort of religious experience had come to him soon after the
death of his brother and his own protracted recuperation.
There, he had explained to the young children, with a fervor
which his daughter Maria had never forgotten, that he had
first attempted to meditate on a phrase their local priest or
svyashchennik had read from the scriptures: "The kingdom
of God is within you".

for them then. Rasputin was the stronger
of the two and while he gradually recovered he had the anguish of watching his
elder brother's strength ebb still further,
until within days he had died.

According to his mother, this death
of his brother Misha cast Rasputin into a
profound depression. But it made his
behavior strange and unpredictable too;
one day he would be off mooning about
in the woods and the next he would be
over-active, shouting and swearing and
getting under her feet. Perhaps, Rasputin
might have been diagnosed today as suffering from a kind of manic-depressive illness. Certainly, it was at about this time that
religion began to enter his life seriously.

But along with the new acknowledgment of
his religious needs and an increasing sense of his
spiritual power, came all too temporal desires and
difficulties. His parents were unsympathetic to this
mystical side in their strange son. His mother was

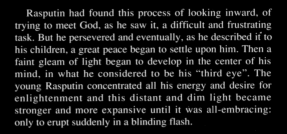

Rasputin had found this process of looking inward, of trying to meet God, as he saw it, a difficult and frustrating task. But he persevered and eventually, as he described it to his children, a great peace began to settle upon him. Then a faint gleam of light began to develop in the center of his mind, in what he considered to be his "third eye". The young Rasputin concentrated all his energy and desire for enlightenment and this distant and dim light became stronger and more expansive until it was all-embracing: only to erupt suddenly in a blinding flash.

uncomprehending and frightened when Rasputin attempted to explain something of what he had experienced. His father, reliant on this only son now for hard labor on the land, was impatient and violent.

Rasputin also, as a young man, had great difficulty with the manic side of his personality; the extreme energy, the sense of being different, being special, the belief that he was called by some greater force but not knowing where, or how, or to what, and the disturbing power of adolescent sexual desires, all exacerbated by surges of uncontrollable energy. All this meant that he became, at times, unmanageable and on the verge of criminality with his excessive drinking and brawling and, so it was rumored, horse-thieving. Rasputin had a reputation also for being sexually precocious, which seems perfectly likely given how well-documented in later life was the extraordinary sexual magnetism that he seemed to possess for women from every walk of life.

The young Rasputin was an ardent seeker, determined to "speak with God" and deeply frustrated by the failures he suffered. In common with many who have experienced enlightenment, Rasputin passed through extraordinary religious experiences.

The Power of Sex

Throughout his adult life, Rasputin's sexual conquests were many and various. His robust libido was just another aspect of his general vitality and lust for living. Singing, dancing, drinking vodka and making love to women were the basic pleasures of peasant life. Particularly so in Siberia's harsh landscape where, for nearly half the year, winter froze the earth and the nights were cold and dark and long. Rasputin, however, seemed to like these pastimes more than most. He shocked the village with his sexual license, but there was never any evidence that any of his female accomplices ever complained.

His manner was straightforward and unpredictable and changed little whether he was propositioning a peasant girl in the fields or a grand lady in St. Petersburg. If he liked the look of a woman in his company he was quite likely to pull her to him, fondle her and start to undo the buttons on her clothes, or, if he was conducting his meetings in his St. Petersburg apartment, he would suggest that she might like to adjourn next door to his room. If a woman seemed at all reluctant or nervous, he would never force his suit; his was an uncomplicated appetite and there were

plenty of willing participants without him having to spare a moment's regret on the few rejections which came his way.

Legend had it that he was a giant of a man, but in fact Rasputin was of no more than average height and stockily built with enormous callused peasant hands. His hair and beard were long and unkempt and his brow furrowed and heavy. But there is no doubt that the most remarkable feature of Rasputin's face was his extraordinarily piercing pale blue eyes. They had a mesmerizing effect on everyone who met him and he was aware of the power of his basilisk stare. His daughter Maria claimed that he could contract and dilate his pupils at will. They were certainly a potent part of his reputation as magician, mystic and sexual magnet.

His daughter claims in her third book of memoirs of her father, that Rasputin had a further outstanding feature which contributed, from his adolescence onwards, to the stories of his great sexual prowess and almost superhuman powers. Stories which were to exacerbate the fear and jealousy of his (male) detractors, in the last rumor-infested years of his life. According to Maria Rasputin, Rasputin had a penis of prodigious size; thirteen inches when erect and, according to another source, with a distinctive and strategically placed wart or mole at the root.

Whatever the truth, Rasputin must have felt a certain pride in his sexual organ, or at least in its symbolic power and reputation, for apparently he

Rasputin did not deny himself the appreciation of women. His belief in the acceptance of beauty and sexual energy led others to point the finger but his own attitude never changed.

was liable, in later years when drunk and asked to prove his identity, to unbutton his flies and wave his penis about in public.

With his youthful exuberance and with so much sexual activity drawing disapproval and malicious gossip on his head from his fellow villagers, it was natural that Rasputin should follow the custom and marry young. He was about nineteen when he went to the neighboring convent of Aballakask for a festival. He met there a striking looking peasant woman from a neighboring village. Her name was Prascovie Dubrovin. She was four years older than he was and had the attractive coloring of blonde hair and very dark eyes. Something about her made Rasputin want to pursue a relationship with her, rather than merely love and leave, as he had before. Perhaps it had something to do with his mother having died. Perhaps his ability to read character had already told him what history was to prove, that here was a young woman who was steady and mature and would work hard on the land and care for the family without complaint, while he sought his destiny in distant countries and with people of another world.

Within six months he had married and brought his new wife to live with himself and his father in Pokrovskoe. His sexual adventures did not stop with his marriage but his wife did not appear to mind; "He has enough to go round" she is reputed to have said philosophically.

Rasputin's spiritual curiosity, however, grew as he listened more attentively

One of Rasputin's great loves was to visit nearby village fêtes and watch or join the dancing and music. It was at such a fête that he met his wife.

A Siberian shaman – like Rasputin, one who has an overwhelming psychological experience which turns him inward and brings him to a life-long path of seeking enlightenment.

The nearby monastery of Verkhotourie – Rasputin would visit regularly the local monks but never showed any sign of desire to renounce the world himself.

to the *startsi*, the wandering holy men who were so much a feature of Russian life. Wandering the vast country, they talked of their travels and discussed the scriptures in return for hospitality from the numerous scattered monasteries and local villagers' homes. The Rasputin house, like every other peasant house, had given food and shelter to many of these men, of differing degrees of holiness and integrity.

Already, by the age of sixteen, Rasputin had visited the nearby monastery of Verkhotourie, which these *startsi* traveled to and from with their tales of the religious life, the relics of St. Simeon, the monastery's patron saint to which they prayed, and the peace and beauty of the buildings set in surrounding woods. Rasputin had to see for himself the community of monks there and all the intriguing detail of the religious way of life. There he also learnt of the hermits, who lived in primitive huts isolated in the forest, the most celebrated of whom was Makari, known throughout Russia for his asceticism and his devotion.

Although increasingly drawn to certain aspects of religion and the spiritual way, Rasputin was never attracted seriously to the idea of becoming a monk and renouncing the outside world. He continued to visit the monastery, however, sometimes alone and sometimes in the company of a friend, the more orthodoxly devout Petcherkin. He took to meditating on the scriptures when he returned home, sometimes breaking into song, and inevitably other villagers would join him in his prayers and discussions.

The most powerful dilemma for Rasputin was the difference between the demands of holiness and the demands of his body - often creating in him depths of despair.

Even as a young man in these humble domestic beginnings, his simple power of religious feeling and expression was noted and drew followers to him. So much so that the local priest began to get suspicious and jealous. He denounced to his superiors these informal meetings at Rasputin's house as "nights of orgy", and the police were called in to investigate.

So afraid was the orthodox church of the influence of breakaway religious sects like the *Khlysty,* that Rasputin's success in attracting a following, mainly of women, provoked the Orthodox imagination with visions of naked, frenetic dancers, indiscriminate coupling of the worshipers and cauldrons of water which steamed and bubbled spontaneously. No doubt to their disappointment, the policemen sent to investigate Rasputin's little gathering found nothing so exotic. In fact one of the men was so impressed by the religious sincerity of Rasputin, by his interpretation of the scriptures and fervor of expression, that he decided to join the small band of worshipers.

Marriage may have provided Rasputin with a more welcoming home and a sympathetic woman to come back to, but it did not change the conduct of his life in any fundamental way. A need to wander was in most Russians' blood, particularly the less well-off classes, and without positions, property and status to fetter them, they would often pack a bundle of a few clothes and minimum food and set off on a week's, a month's, a year's pilgrimage from monastery to town, or just traversing the vast empty spaces of their country, stopping as they chose, going where they willed.

Sex and Spirit

Stranniki and *startsi*, wandering holy men, had been a colorful feature of village life since Rasputin had been old enough to notice these ragged men with their thrilling tales of distant lands and customs. He too would take off for a few months, staying at monasteries and discussing the scriptures and then moving on. Rasputin's instinctive self had little trouble reconciling his hearty appetites for vodka-drinking, dancing and sex, with his religious sensibilities. However, away from home and meditating on various interpretations of the scriptures, there came a time in his young adulthood when Rasputin, in attempting to live a chaste life for the sake of the spiritual, came close to despair. His daughter's memoirs relate the characteristic way that he came to reconcile the two apparently contradictory forces in his own nature.

On one of his meditative wanderings, Rasputin had been tormented by his unassuaged sexual desire and was plagued by thoughts and images which completely thwarted his attempts to pray. Exhausted, sleepless, in despair, his attention was caught by the achingly sweet birdsong in the tree above him. Looking up, he saw the little bird, a male, serenading his female. The liquid beauty of his song, so reminiscent of the spiritual ecstasy that Rasputin so sought and seemed to be denied, was a direct result of the bird's courtship, of its desire. Suddenly, it seemed to Rasputin, he held the key to his terrible dilemma. If this bird with his celestial song was moved by desire, how could it be evil? This was the answer to his prayers, a sign from Nature itself, from God's own world.

One of the great turning points in Rasputin's sexual dilemma was taken after making love with three women he came across bathing in a pond. God did not strike him down and his prayers thereafter were clearer and more powerful than ever before.

Rasputin's struggle between sex and religion might have been alleviated had he known more of the Tantrikas.

The story continued with Rasputin, elated by this recent revelation, wandering on through the forest drawn by the sound of laughter. In a clearing he came across three young women bathing naked in a small lake. Without the slightest hesitation or reservation, he cast off his clothes and joined them in the pool. After much frolicking and horseplay, so the story goes, Rasputin then made love to each of them in turn on the grassy bank.

According to his daughter's account, that night he was able to pray for the first time in weeks and with a fervor and clarity that convinced him that he had managed to integrate that day, the demands of the spirit with the no less noble, demands of the flesh. This incident saw the birth of Rasputin's philosophy of spiritual awakening through sexual fulfillment, a philosophy he was to propagate and live by for the rest of his life.

His argument was simple. God had made man, and sexual desire was an essential part of man's nature. Just as a just God would never punish man for assuaging his thirst with a draught of cool water, so he could not punish him for assuaging his sexual desire through straightforward sexual congress. (Rasputin did not seem to think that homosexuality was approved of by God.) Man not only desires; he is the product of desire. Without sex, Rasputin argued, God's universe would be devoid of all animal life, and therefore of humanity and religion.

The stranniki, pilgrims or wanderers were an important feature of Russian life and imagination. Some men in their late middle age would distribute what they had to their children and, taking up a staff and a bundle, set off to wander until death eventually caught up with them. Others would have periods, when they were young perhaps, when they would set off without warning, and with a faraway look in their eyes, to explore the challenge of the unknown.

The Peasant Inheritance

Rasputin's religious feelings did not modify his sexual behavior, nor did they appear to change the way he conducted his daily life. His exuberant appetite for sensation of all kinds meant he continued in his young adulthood, and even after his marriage, to be thought of in the village as a trouble-maker; a drinker, a womanizer, a brawler. His restlessness and seeking after excess, both deeply ingrained characteristics of his people, led him into trouble and drew, sometimes, grudging admiration. There was something full-blooded and manly about his wild, drunken rides through the village, whooping and galloping hell-for-leather into the night. His fighting the men and seducing the women, reaffirmed the Siberian peasants' pride in the lustiness, recklessness and strength of their menfolk. But there were at least two incidents when Rasputin's recklessness meant he fell foul of the law.

For a time in the 1890's Rasputin supplemented his income by working as a carter. On one of his trips, one of the horses which drew the cart and belonged to the contractor went missing. Rasputin was immediately suspected of horse-thieving, a common and serious crime. The police were

Rasputin spent a short time in the jail of the local city of Tobolsk for neglecting a shipment of furs.

called in and found twenty-one roubles in Rasputin's pockets. This was a large sum of money and seemed to be proof enough that he had taken the horse and sold it. Rasputin, however, denied the charge vehemently. The money had been given to him by the monastery of Verkhotourie, where he had spent three months working and praying alongside the monks. The horse, he claimed, had broken away from its restraining rope at night and had slipped into the flood-swollen river and been drowned. The circumstances looked suspicious but the case was dismissed eventually for lack of evidence.

This episode was followed too closely by another suspicious disappearance of property. Rasputin was in charge of delivering by wagon a consignment of furs to the local town of Tyumen. He had left the cargo untended while he took a break at midday, and a good quantity of vodka, no doubt was also consumed. But rather than admit to his negligence, Rasputin made up a story of how he had been attacked by robbers: after a fierce fight, with him alone against their many, they had made off with the booty. This story did not convince the law and he was sentenced at Tobolsk on February 14, 1891 to a flogging and a short term of imprisonment.

There is a vivid account by Kartashev, a neighbor of his in Pokrovskoe, of Rasputin's opportunist thieving. It is revealing in the violence of Rasputin's threat when apprehended, and the extreme brutality of the neighbor's response.

"I caught Grigori stealing pieces of my fence. He broke them up and put the sticks on his cart and was about to tie them up and take them away when I caught him and ordered him to come to the village elder with the stolen property. When he refused, and in order to get away tried to hit me with his axe, I gave him such a blow with my pitchfork that the blood poured from his nose and mouth and he fell to the ground unconscious. At first I thought I'd killed him, but when he began to move I brought him round and took him to the elder. He didn't want to go but I hit him a few more times in the face, and then he went of his own accord."

After this beating and a further absence at the monastery, there was some evidence that Rasputin returned a very different man. His unbridled excesses seemed to have disappeared. He had given up meat and was not to drink Vodka again until the height of his fame in St. Petersburg found him succumbing once more to the peasant tradition of reckless drinking bouts. His manner and way of speaking seemed so distracted, that the neighbor Kartashev believed the blow he had dealt him must have damaged his brain.

Rasputin's speech had become rapid and fragmented and sometimes so garbled that he became incomprehensible to others.

He appeared much more nervous and wary, loath to look people straight in the eye, but when he did, meeting their curious gaze with a wild, staring expression which could be alarming. The depressive mania to which he might well have been prone, seemed to have been exacerbated during this time away; he would alternate between moods of wild exaltation and the deepest depressions, when his thoughts seemed turned inwards in some terrible struggle. The monks had taught him to read, however, and write a little, although he was never to become absolutely proficient in either.

Domestically, things appeared stable. His wife was a stoic and tolerant woman who produced, without much difficulty or delay, their first baby, a son. There is little doubt that Rasputin was a fond and proud father, if often absent and increasingly unlike other fathers. He was overjoyed by the advent of this first son, by the creation of his very own family. And so when this little child died suddenly and inexplicably at the age of six months, Rasputin was devastated by his loss. He could not understand why. Had God forsaken him? Was it some bitter sign that he had done wrong? What was the meaning of this destruction of a blameless life, of a child so beloved by his parents?

In his despair, he set off once more for the monastery of Verkhotourie to see the omniscient hermit Makari. There in the forest, Rasputin found the old monk at prayer and he sat at a distance and waited for him to finish. They talked. They prayed together. Makari told him that only those who came to know God would understand the meaning of their suffering. And

The hermit Makari at the monastery of Verkhotourie helped Rasputin on his path to understanding the nature of his suffering – a significant stepping stone on the pathway he sought.

Rasputin's path to enlightenment was to contain many visions and in particular the Black Virgin Mary was to figure strongly amongst them. The Black Virgins are symbols of power and majesty – the opposite aspect to the traditional Madonna's maidenhead or tender maternity – a pagan sexual goddess that much more appealed to the physical concept of Rasputin's enlightenment. They personified the Holy Grail and the Ark of the Covenant, in a quest for lost feminine wisdom and the ardent search for the soul.

feeling that Makari, more than any other mortal being, had helped him on his spiritual way, Rasputin took his leave of him with gratitude. He went home again strengthened and consoled.

He returned to the routine of working on the land alongside his father and praying for enlightenment. He did not have to wait for long. One day, in the middle of ploughing their field, Rasputin came to the end of a furrow and paused to look up. The sky was lit with a peculiar radiance, and as he gazed into this light he was amazed to see the image of the Virgin Mary

before him, veiling the sun. She appeared to be sweeping her hand towards the distant horizon, gesturing as if she wanted Rasputin to follow the way she pointed. Rasputin closed his eyes, and opened them again to find the vision was still there. The Virgin was swathed in garments unlike any he had ever seen depicted in the numerous ikons he had studied at monasteries and churches he had come across in his travels. Rasputin fell to his knees in prayer. When he looked up again into the sky the vision had gone. Immediately he fetched some wood, nailed it into a makeshift cross, and pushed it into the ploughed earth to mark where he had been standing when this remarkable vision had been revealed to him.

His first thought was to tell his friend Petcherkin, who had shared some

The moment o, one of Rasputi, most significa, visions occurr, as he ploughe, and came to t, end of a furro, Looking up, h, saw the Virgin, Mary before h, veiling the su,

The city of Tobolsk, visited often by Rasputin primarily to come to the monastery where he was well known to the monks.

of his spiritual explorations and had already claimed he had a vocation to become a monk. Together, they decided to return to the monastery to ask the hermit Makari what this revelation meant.

After their day's journey on foot, the two eager peasants found the hermit. They described to him what Rasputin had seen in his field at home. Makari confirmed what Rasputin and his friend had hoped – that this was a sign that God had some great work for Rasputin to do and that he had to prepare to go on a long pilgrimage. Makari then told him he would have to go to Mount Athos in Greece and pray there for further guidance.

Rasputin knew that this must be a very long way away, over difficult and dangerous terrain. He knew that he would be traveling through unknown lands where unknown languages were spoken. He knew he would have no food with him and little clothing. No comfort or luxury could be afforded him except the knowledge that he was doing God's will and that something important had been assigned to him. In fact Mount Athos lay more than 2000 miles to the south and west of the small Siberian settlement that had been home to Rasputin, for more than twenty years. The journey would have to be on foot, would mean crossing great mountain ranges with little evidence of habitation and little chance of shelter. With the equally arduous return journey, the whole expedition would take more than two years. Rasputin went home to tell his father and his wife what it was he had to do.

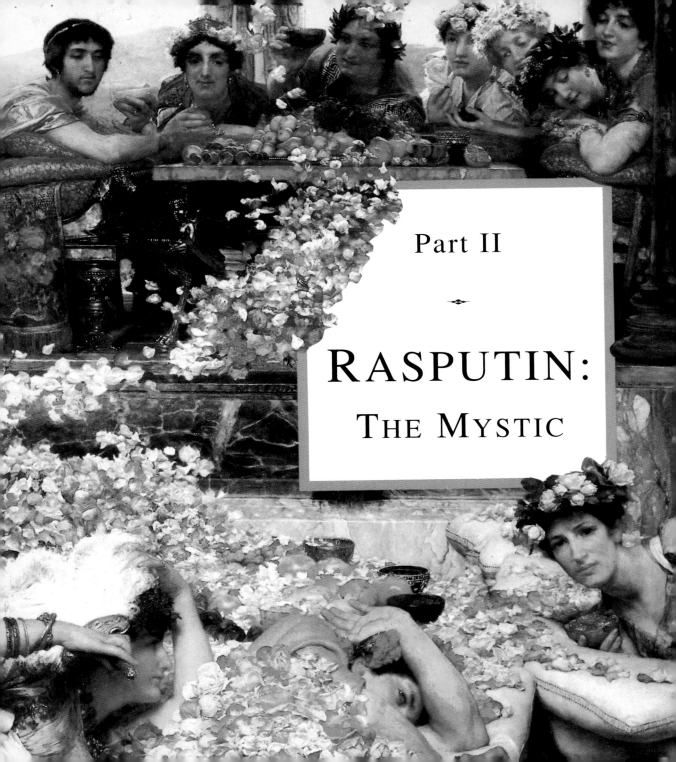

Part II

❖

RASPUTIN:
THE MYSTIC

Sects & Sex

Rasputin's spiritual nature and aspirations cannot be discussed without some knowledge of the religious influences and traditions in which he was steeped. The powerful drives of his own nature were central also, in explaining the theory and form of worship that would most attract him. Until the middle of the 17th century, Orthodox Christianity prevailed in Russia. Religion was not an intense issue until the 1650's when the newly appointed Patriarch Nikon began to forcibly reform the Church. He demanded that priests and religion should be awarded a much more powerful position in Russian society. He also set out to change certain details in the service and prayer book, most very trivial, for instance decreeing that three fingers, not two, should be used when crossing oneself. His plans were enforced with a brutality and barbarity to which some of his flock, perhaps previously lethargic about their faith, responded to with equal barbarity.

Many hundreds, even thousands, of Old Believers – as they came to be called – chose martyrdom, murder and suicide, often with grotesque methods and in mass movements, to express their outrage at the harshness of the

The Great Red Dragon and the Woman clothed with the Sun – by William Blake. The Dragon was symbol of the devil and the painting as a whole represented the bizarre nature of the darker side of God.

repression of their unreformed brand of Orthodoxy, and their desire to die rather than endure these enforced changes. They escaped, as far as they could, the jurisdiction of the State by traveling to the furthest reaches of the empire and setting up communities and monasteries there. Siberia, vast, inhospitable and neglected would always be a shelter for criminals, outsiders and dissidents of all kinds; and for those persecuted for their religious practices and beliefs it seemed a place of respite. This schism, and the violence of the Church's persecution of the schismatics, set up a bitterness that cast its shadow down the centuries. It also weakened the spiritual and temporal authority of the Orthodox Church and prepared the ground for the flourishing of the many breakaway sects which practiced their religion in varying degrees of unorthodoxy.

The sectarianism that flourished, and was a central part of the religious landscape when Rasputin was exploring his own spiritual impulses, was born of the peasant culture, springing from the peasants' own needs, superstitions and experience. There was no authority to hand down doctrinal truths.

The sects, some of them bizarre, essentially pagan, with barely a Christian element to them, were as various as the individuals who were drawn to them. The fervor that they engendered in their followers, along with the hatred of the established Church, was the only common characteristic.

There were two sects in particular, the *Khlysty* (translated to mean the Flagellants, or possibly the Christs) and the *Skoptsi* (the Eunuchs), which were rumored to be more widely followed and to have strong constituencies in Siberia. Rumors and suspicions and scandalous stories were rife around these sects, especially as their practices were sensational, and necessarily kept secret except to the initiates. Their power was also greatly feared by the Orthodox Church.

These sects were seen as the dark side of the Russian soul; an expression of something primitive, heretical, profane. The emotional abandonment, even licentiousness, of some of their practices added to the fear that here existed a dark and ungovernable force which had to be suppressed. To the followers of these sects the threat of draconian punishments was a real one.

Rasputin had heard the rumors of their practices and had come across some of their followers and even, according to his daughter, for a time had joined the *Khlysty*. There are some claims that this heretical movement existed as long ago as the 14th century, but its history is charted from the early 17th century, when it was founded by another peasant with outstanding powers of oratory, Danilo Filipov. He produced a bible, called the Dove Book, which stated that men should not marry, and if married should abandon their wives and call their children "sins". A follower of the cult could then take a "spiritual wife" but any sexual relations with her were forbidden. Swearing and alcohol similarly were forbidden, and martyrdom was the perfect resolution.

Pagan sects in Russia were powerful enough to frighten the established Church, with their secret membership and scandalous practices – seen as the dark side of the Russian soul and expressing something primitive and profane.

The licentious practices and the evident enjoyment by members of the activities of the pagan cults, gave rise to fears amongst the established Church of ungovernable forces.

Such ungovernable forces clearly needed suppressing, for those who feared their own temptation!

The central belief, however, was that Christ did not return to Heaven when he died but inhabited another body and continued his work on Earth. In this way, they believed there were many Christs and that the original one was no holier than the subsequent ones. Filipov, naturally, was considered to be one of these Christs.

Their methods of worship, and the secrecy with which the followers protected the sect through the centuries from persecution, were what provoked the excited rumors in fashionable circles, and the prurient interest and fear of the Church. Prince Yusupov, Rasputin's future assassin, described an evening of worship for a *Khlyst* gathering. The general facts (if not the tone) are supported in a similar account, by Rasputin's daughter Maria.

"The faithful used to assemble by night in a hut or forest clearing, lit by hundreds of tapers. The purpose of these *radenie* ceremonies, was to create a religious ecstasy, an erotic frenzy. After invocations and hymns, the faithful formed a ring and began to sway in rhythm, then to whirl round and round, spinning faster and faster. As a state of dizziness was essential to the 'divine flux', the master of ceremonies flogged any dancer whose vigor abated. The *radenie* ended in a horrible orgy, everyone rolling on the ground in ecstasy or in convulsions. They preached that he who is possessed by the spirit belongs not to himself, but to the spirit who controls him and who is responsible for all his actions and for any sins he may commit." What Yusupov alluded to was the indiscriminate sexual intercourse

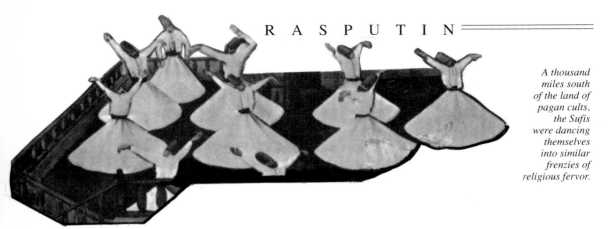

A thousand miles south of the land of pagan cults, the Sufis were dancing themselves into similar frenzies of religious fervor.

which, according to Maria Rasputin and other commentators, followed on, and which often resulted in incest and homosexuality.

There are two points of particular note in this account. The first being the parallel between this sect's belief that in a state of religious ecstasy (or even physical abandonment) one is not responsible for one's actions and the Russian law itself, that held that in a state of drunkenness one similarly abdicated responsibility. Perhaps this meant that in the Russian psyche there lurked a belief that in certain states it was justifiable to relinquish one's everyday curbs and restraints; that one could abandon oneself to one's senses and not be held responsible for anything that may transpire.

The other point of note, is just how much this ecstatic abandonment was a part of Rasputin's own nature. As a young man his sensation-seeking had got him into trouble with his drinking, fighting and fornicating. All his life his love of dancing would sometimes overcome him and he would dance until exhausted. Even in the middle of religious meetings he would sometimes be so moved that he would break into song and start dancing the old peasant dances he had learnt as a youth. This love of emotional expression and generally excessive behavior, was what kept Rasputin from ever submitting to the discipline of the monastery and the life of a monk. This love of sensation, and his inability and unwillingness to renounce his sexual needs, was to attract him to the *Khlysty*, romanticized by rumors of their intemperate, forbidden practices.

Khlysty & Skoptsi

Maria Rasputin recounted a story of how Rasputin was initiated into the *Khlysty* while he was in one of his periods of wandering and meditating. He had already been exposed to hushed discussions of the sect's beliefs when at the monastery of Verkhotourie, where, it had been rumored, some of the monks were secret practitioners of this heresy. But it was not until Rasputin came across a poor peasant family on his wanderings that he attended his first *Khlyst* gathering. He had knocked on the door of a humble peasant dwelling asking for some food, as many pilgrims had done at his home and as he was to do many times again. There he discovered that the family were in despair over their daughter, who was ill and did not seem to be recovering. Rasputin prayed by her bedside until the child began to stir and passed the crisis of her illness. Over a celebration meal, the family asked him about his religious beliefs and eventually came round to the question of whether he led a life of chastity, as most holy men were expected to do.

Rasputin's answer that he did not think chastity was important to the spiritual life, emboldened the mother of the sick child to ask him if he might be one of the *Khlysty*. When she heard that he was not, yet was interested by their doctrines, she became anxious lest she had already said too much. Only their leader could break the vow of secrecy and explain their philosophy and rites to an outsider. Her gratitude to Rasputin for his apparently miraculous healing of her daughter, together with his obviously sincere interest in the sect, decided her to introduce this unusual pilgrim to their leader.

In the deep dark woods of Rasputin's times, the peasants indulged in erotic radenie ceremonies. Much of this secret pagan activity dominated Russian peasant life.

When Rasputin heard the leader's eloquent justifica- tion for the sect's belief, that through expressing man's carnal nature with- out guilt, he came closer to God, Rasputin recognized with relief and some excitement how closely this resembled his own experience. It was a knowledge, however, achieved only after the most painful struggle between the orthodox teach- ings of the Church on one side and his own conscience, his nature and needs, on the other. With some anticipation, Rasputin set off that night in the company of the parents of the child he had just cured, for the secret ren- dezvous with the *Khlysty*.

Off the beaten track, deep in the woods, they came to an isolated and apparently disused barn. Entering through a door at the back, they found some dirt steps cut into the earth which led to an underground dug-out room. Giving the coded knock on the door, they were let into the lamp-lit meeting and the ritual began. Until that moment, Rasputin had only known about these secret rites through local gossip and the lurid rumors that intrigued every strata of Russian society. Here at last, he was participating in something that had been kept alive for centuries, despite brutal suppres- sion and persecution, through the fanaticism and fervor of its followers. Here was something combining eroticism and religion, excitement and dan- ger: Rasputin was bound to be hooked.

There were ten people present, only three of whom were men. The evening began straightforwardly enough with prayers from the Orthodox litany and for a time everything seemed familiar. But then the leader began to talk about "the highest worship of God" and how each of them was an incarnation of God and therefore should love and worship each other. They were then all admonished to love one another. This was the sign for every one to remove their robes and begin to dance, utterly naked, in a circle around the leader. The dancing grew faster and more abandoned, they were whirling round and round in an increasing frenzy of ecstasy and exhaustion. Then at the height of the dancing a woman broke away from the group with a wild cry and cast herself upon the leader and immediately engaged him in copulation. The group collapsed to the ground and proceeded with indiscriminate and orgiastic sexual intercourse. Outnumbered more than three to one by women, Rasputin set to with a will. Nothing could make him happier than to be able to combine the two great impulses of his nature without guilt.

Rasputin's happiness was completed, so his daughter related, when the next morning he fell to his knees in prayer and found that it came to him as clearly and sweetly as ever. God had not been displeased by the activities of the previous night. He and the *Khlysty* were right in believing that God approved of the appetites he had given to man, and that denial of these basic needs interfered with the free expression of man's spiritual nature.

The orgiastic rituals combined with alcohol and sexual indulgence were more a way of life than ever they are today.

An even more extreme heretic sect which Rasputin would have known of, and even met adherents of, but was unlikely to have ever been personally involved with, was the *Skoptsi,* or the Mutilants. This was a development of the *Khlysty* and judged a man or woman's closeness to Christ by his or her ability to bear physical pain. The founder of the *Khlysty* was supposed to have been crucified twice, his successor, as a sign of advanced spirituality, three times, each time with more horrific detail than the first. The founder of the *Skoptsi* went further still and decreed that men should be castrated and women should have their breasts amputated and their genitals mutilated. The founder emasculated himself with a red-hot iron.

Exaggerated rumors and allegation abounded about both sects; sex, the repression or licentious expression of, seemed to dominate the doctrines and make them of even greater interest to outsiders. Even the *Skoptsi,* which one might have thought free of the accusations of sexual license that were leveled at the *Khlysty,* were reputed to engage in orgies, the men, who were meant to castrate themselves, often not committing the full mutilation. These were by no means the strangest or most grotesque of the sects which Rasputin would have known about and come across in his travels. They are significant in giving some indication of the amount of fervor, hysteria, rumor and prurience which surrounded these cults, and explain some of the awe, fascinated fear and accusations of satanic practices which were to follow Rasputin during his period of greatest influence in the Court.

The doctrine of the *Khlysty* with its alternation between chastity and denial and an ecstatic licentiousness appealed directly to Rasputin's extreme nature. These opposing forces in his character had caused him times great unhappiness but now he had justification for expressing them b

Rasputin determined then and there to become a member of this se sect and even to become a leader, a *vozhd*, in his own right. Many follow were to marvel at his forceful eloquence, at the sense of being in the prese of an extraordinary man. Never educated or refined in manner, Rasp nevertheless, aroused even in his detractors a grudging recognition of charismatic power. He was "both coarse and eloquent, hypocritical, fana and holy, a sinner and an ascetic, a womanizer who put on an act for e minute of the day, arousing curiosity, wielding great influence and enjoyi knowledge of his fellow men that was tantamount to clairvoyance."

It was women, although not exclusively so, who were most respon to his mesmeric power. There were to be many, during his lifetime and a his death, who had been involved in similar rites with him and wer believe that he was another Christ, the Christ that the *Khlysty* claimed l

The extraordinary religious passion that surrounded Rasputin's life and times, resulted perhaps even in the supposition amongst his followers and devotees, that he was a Christ figure himself.

The Pilgrimage

With the vision of the Virgin before him and the words of the hermit Makari echoing in his ears, Rasputin knew that at last he had been called by God for some special purpose. It was the early 1890's and Rasputin was in his twenties. All his undirected religious yearnings, his experiments with his faith, his lapses, his inchoate hopes of a life and influence beyond the steppes of his homeland, all were soothed now by the security of the knowledge that he was a Chosen One, and he focused on the terrific pilgrimage to Mount Athos that lay ahead.

His long-suffering wife was reluctant to let him go so far and for so long, particularly as she had her suspicions that she might be pregnant again. But she recognized how central to his life was a sense of recognition from his God. Prascovie Dubrovin Rasputin knew that nothing could stop her husband from going; she could only give him her blessing. His father was much less tolerant and grumbled generally around the village that Grisha had taken up being a pilgrim of God so that he could get out of the farmwork – hadn't he always been an odd one? Always lazy and wanting to go off on his own. This was the last straw!

A few days later, Rasputin set off on the longest pilgrimage of his life.

His faithful friend, Petcherkin, had begged to be able to accompany him and so the two, with a bundle of clothes and no more provisions than would keep them for a few days, turned towards the south-west and the distant Ural mountains, rising in some places to 5,000 feet. These two young peasants were to follow a tradition which was well-worn through the centuries, and accepted by the Russian people as a common, and commendable urge, to wander with neither money nor possessions and preaching any religious teachings that came to mind. In the process such a wandering pilgrim was trying to find his soul.

Rasputin and his friend covered on average perhaps ten miles a day. They would knock on the doors of peasants' homes along the way to ask for food and shelter. But in the short, hot summers would manage to glean a quantity of food from the woodland and fields that they passed through. At night they would sleep under the stars. People everywhere were as hospitable as the villagers had been back home in Pokrovskoe. They would be invited in to join the family meal. Their stories of their travels and far-off places would repay the material generosity offered them. If the villager so wished, they could pray alongside Rasputin and Petcherkin, and discuss the scriptures or ask advice.

Inevitably Rasputin came across people who were ill and dying. He would kneel and pray by their beds with the peculiar concentration and fervor that could make him exhausted and drenched in a cold sweat. There

were many times when he appeared to cure, or heal, or bring relief to terrible suffering, and when the family fell to their knees in gratitude he would tell them, "It's God's doing, not mine." His reputation, though, began to spread.

There were many monasteries along the way and the friends would visit them for conversation, hospitality and to say Mass with the monks. Over the Urals, down the mighty River Volga, around the shores of the Black Sea and then south through Rumania and Bulgaria to Greece; it was a trip that lasted more than ten months and had moments of great hardship, fear, hunger, and cold. Rasputin was always easily moved by the splendors of nature and, after the difficult and barren terrain of much of their journey, he must have been struck by the lush beauty of the area of Khalkidhiki in Greece, from which projected the finger of land on which Mount Athos rose over 6000 feet sheer above the sea.

His own writing on contemplating a sunset on a later pilgrimage to the Holy Land expresses something of what he might have felt gazing out over the Aegean Sea for the first time.

"Magnificent it is indeed when the sun descends over the sea and sets amid shimmering beams. Who can tell the value of these resplendent beams which warm and caress the soul and give healing consolation. The sun gradually sets over the hills and the heart of man is filled with wondering sadness at the marvel of those glittering rays – then it begins to get dark."

The silent and inspiring Monastery of Mount Athos overlooked the sea in an awesome beauty, that would be sufficient to excite the spiritual aspirations of any traveler.

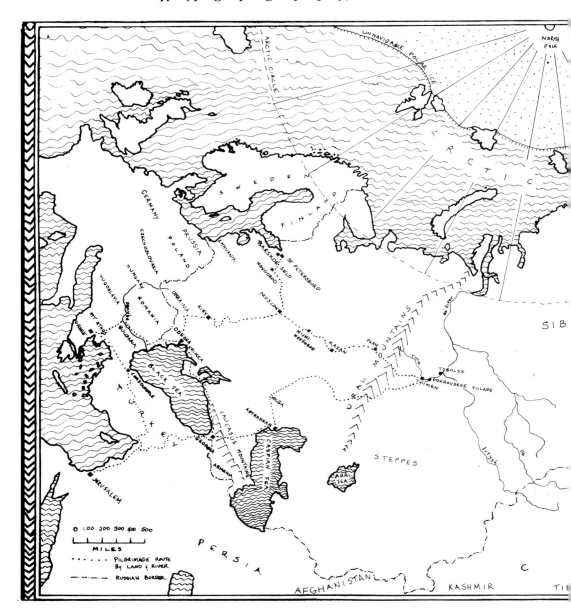

The Pilgrim Route

In order for us to appreciate the immensity of the pilgrimage undertaken by Rasputin, we need to appreciate the incredible size of the country he inhabited. To cross Russia on such a journey might take an entire life-time and might also, still more likely, end that life-time. Rasputin and his friend Petcherkin moved at the rate of perhaps ten miles a day on this trip – a snail's pace over mountains that stood often 5,000 feet high!

Mount Athos was and remained a strange anomaly. The peninsular of land was scattered with numerous large monasteries, some picturesquely and precariously perched on the steep, rocky cliffs, pendant over the sea. Revered as the holy center of the Orthodox Church, there was an attempt to insulate the whole area from carnal temptation by forbidding access to women, and by selecting only male animals to live there. All men who wished to enter the sacred mountain were required to grow beards as a visible mark of their mature masculinity. (Eunuchs, along with women, were banned.)

At first Rasputin was overjoyed to be at the heart of his religion, surrounded by the cream of holy men. His friend Petcherkin immediately pursued his long-held vocation to become a monk and prepared to take his vows. But Rasputin was not long on this holy mountain before he came across a couple of monks in the woods obviously involved in some homosexual practice. This sight so shocked him that it turned him forever from the place. "There is nothing here but dirt, vermin and moral filth!" he railed at his friend, but could not deter him from staying. Rasputin, however, for the rest of his life, was to dismiss the whole community of Mount Athos as a hotbed of unnatural vice.

Rasputin passed through the magnificent city of Constantinople on his journey to the Holy Land.

Even writing of his visit to Jerusalem, Rasputin noticed that apart from the pilgrims, there were many there who exploited or disgraced God's name; and even there, the holiest of cities, the vices of Mount Athos could be found. "It is the monks of Athos who offend most," he wrote in his memoirs, "and therefore, they ought not to be allowed there...It is difficult to explain, but those who have been there will know."

After Rasputin's disillusionment with the heart of the Orthodox Church, there is some dispute as to where he went next. He may well have set off alone on his return journey and wandered for about a year around western Siberia, preaching, healing the sick, joining in the *Khlyst* practices in secret, and meditating and praying for further enlightenment on what his spiritual task might be. However, his daughter remembered her father's magical tales of his pilgrimage and claims that Rasputin then turned to the Holy Land in search of his God. It seems quite probable that having realized that the monastic life most definitely was not for him, Rasputin left Greece with the intention of traveling on to the Holy Land in search of further spiritual clarification. He was to make another visit about twenty years later when he was established at St Petersburg and at the height of his fame. His *Thoughts and Meditations* were notes of what he saw then. Ecstatic as his descriptions were, he did write "It is best to visit Jerusalem only once to see all the places and to realize their worth...The first time you see them, you are overcome by

The Holy Land formed the crucible for Rasputin's faith, almost like a war hero telling the tall tales of his exploits, Rasputin would recount again and again the passion and pleasure of his pilgrimage.

Placed so often at the very top of a single block of mountainous stone, the monasteries brought a silence exposed only to the gaze of God.

The Black Virgin, a mirror image of the somewhat more placid and untouchable white version. The black goddess signified power and passion, more appropriate to the times of Russia in Rasputin's age.

a joy beyond un-
the second time,
cize, then unbelief
derstanding, but
you begin to criti-
comes upon you."
which suggests that he had made a previous visit. He tended to describe only
his own experiences and not to speculate about other people's.

Having been on the road continuously, in poverty and discomfort, with
neither a base nor sufficient food nor clean clothes, often in danger, for
almost a year, Rasputin showed great hardiness of body and spirit in press-
ing on further south for another 1000 miles of an even more difficult journey. There is no record of what he saw or thought on that first visit, but his
daughter remembered the affectionate detail and the spiritual excitement
with which her father retold many times his experiences and adventures
while in the Holy Land, the crucible of his faith.

Rasputin returned at length, almost two and a half years after he had
first set out from his own village of Pokrovskoe. He wandered up through
Siberia, revisiting the monasteries he had seen on his outward journey. At
Kazan, Rasputin was overjoyed to see, for the first time, the painting of the
Black Virgin of Kazan, exactly like the vision he had seen in the fields,
when he had been struck by the Virgin's dark raiment, so unlike anything
he had seen before.

Stopping at these monasteries gave him a longed-for few days' rest from
the road and the chance of some company and some spiritual solace.

Pilgrims waiting to cross the Dnieper to Kiev. The whole ethos of the Russian pilgrimage was almost a way of life for thousands, who would undertake the vast journeys of spiritual accomplishment.

The extraordinary city of Kazan , where Rasputin finally faced the painting of the Black Virgin of Kazan, exactly she whom he had seen in his vision in the ploughed field.

Rasputin would pray with the monks, take Mass, eat well and in return recount his experiences and religious revelations of the intervening years. He could join up once more with the *Khlysty* and express again his appetite for sensation and excess.

After so long away from home, so many spiritual and temporal experiences, so much time alone to meditate and confront the raw essence of himself, Rasputin did appear to be a changed man. Inevitably he had grown much leaner and was more disheveled. But there was a greater authority about his manner, a stronger sense of his own spirituality and calling. His extraordinarily piercing blue eyes, seemed all the more mesmerizing as they blazed from his weather-beaten face. He looked nearer forty than thirty, for the hardships, the wind and sun and burning cold had taken their toll. People he met no longer thought of him as just a pilgrim, a *strannik*, as he seemed to exude the much greater gravitas and wisdom of a *starets*, a wandering holy man.

His reputation as a healer and teacher, had preceded him, although no one in his own village suspected that the new holy man being talked about, was none other than the wild man of Pokrovskoe, Grigori Efimovich Rasputin.

His wife had no idea where he was, when he would be back, or even if he was still alive, and so when a tall, bedraggled pilgrim came to her door

At the end of the incredible two and a half year pilgrimage Rasputin had matured into a different person. Rid of the excesses of vodka and the painful dilemmas of his physical and spiritual duality, he was a fulfilled man as though finally having found a way to use his extraordinary energies.

A Siberian village close to home once more, as Rasputin returned from his vast pilgrimage.

asking for food and shelter, she bustled to the kitchen to prepare something for him to eat, as she had for hundreds of itinerants before him. It was only as she set the food down before him and she heard him speak that she recognized her long-lost husband.

The story of Rasputin's return was obviously one which was repeated with much amusement and pleasure within the family, for years to come. Prascovie, his wife, immediately flew into his arms, amazed at how thin he had grown, how long was his beard; how strange to have the years roll back in just one moment and to find herself again in his embrace. She then proudly brought forward her surprise, their son, Dmitri, born while Rasputin was away and now a sturdy toddler of nearly two.

Rasputin, although so often absent, appeared to have been a good, affectionate and proud father and husband. Throughout his life he was to embrace, if fleetingly, hundreds of women. He was to be worshipped by some as the true Christ, and sought out by others as a sexual legend. He was to be awarded tremendous power over the affairs of a vast country, and yet, for Rasputin there was no woman with whom he appeared to be in any way emotionally involved – apart from that blonde-haired girl he had made his wife when he was only nineteen. After the tragedy of his first baby's death, the joy in having another son at last, meant, he thought, that God had somehow brought his first son back to him.

The Beginnings
of Influence

The moment the villagers of Pokrovskoe knew that Rasputin had returned after a pilgrimage of more than two years, they flocked to his house to inquire how he was and hear his stories of all he had seen and done. They too were impressed by the changes his experiences had wrought on him. Rasputin no longer ate meat; more extraordinarily, he had eschewed vodka, and would do so for many years to come. When he talked on religious matters there was an intensity and depth to his conviction and manner that riveted his audience. He had not seen it as necessary to take a vow of chastity, however, and that aspect of his life would continue unfettered, but enhanced with a religious rationale.

Rasputin would succumb to his desires and rationalize his behavior by expounding the *Khlyst* philosophy that we are all Christs and should love one another; that God made man, lust and all, and therefore how can satisfying this God-given appetite be considered a sin. He used a different tack with his women disciples: in order to be absolved from sin, one first had to sin. How much more spiritually enriched were those who had sinned, and been forgiven, than those who had never sinned at all?

With the ascendancy of his religious feeling, combined later with his presence in the sophisticated society of St. Petersburg, he devised another theory about the flesh and the spirit. Rasputin was prone to testing the self-control of himself and the women he desired (or who desired him). In these periods self-control rather than self-indulgence seemed preferable.

*Once home
~ain, Rasputin
is seen here
~h some of his
~ollowers and
devotees,
~ostly women,
~any of whom
would also
have been
~ual partners.*

Rasputin liked to "test" himself by undressing with one or more women. These naked women would then wash him – and wash with him – soaping his genitals and testing his fortitude to the full. Then would follow bed, with Rasputin, sandwiched between desirable female flesh, claiming he was to spend the night resisting his desires, and exhorting the women to resist theirs. He (and they) were intermittently successful. But these later sophistications were yet to come. In those heady days after his return from Mount Athos and the Holy Land, he drew a large gathering of his fellow villagers to the house, initially for stories of his adventures, but increasingly a hard core began to meet at his house for prayers. Rasputin's strength was always to be his powerful peasant mentality. Even through the corridors of power, he remained always a man of the people, talking in simple and direct language about ideas and emotions they could understand. He never really allied himself with the theory and dogma of the Orthodox Church, never became removed from the primitive, superstitious, intuitive mind of the Siberian peasant, with his lack of respect for authority,

A specially built secret underground chapel, similar to Rasputin's. Such places of worship were commonly built and normally unknown to others.

With the regular meetings of villagers who wanted to pray with him, and sometimes bring their sick, Rasputin decided to build a place of worship. Like Christ, he said he would go to the stable, and so he and some men from the village began to dig an underground room in the soil under the barn on his farm, that sheltered the horses.

Just as the old village priest had objected to any competition from Rasputin in the days before his calling, so the new one, Father Peter, was angered by the following that this self-styled *starets* seemed to be attracting from his own congregation. It was not only professional pride which was involved; money also might be lost if his parishioners decided not to be married, baptized or buried in his church. Besides, there was something suspicious about this underground chamber – and about the number of women who seemed to be particularly devoted followers. Rumor had it that the *Khlysty* carried on their debauched practices in subterranean chapels. Perhaps, the priest thought, Rasputin was the *vozhd* of a sectarian group in the heart of his village.

When denouncing Rasputin from the pulpit as a devil seemed to do little to diminish his appeal, the hard-pressed priest decided to appeal to his bishop at Tobolsk. Once again, a deputation of churchmen and police could find little to complain of in the way Rasputin conducted his meetings. In fact, some of the members of the investigating team came away deeply impressed by the sincerity of the *starets* and the very real good he seemed to be doing, his healing ability being attested to by many.

The ancient and beautiful city of Kiev was one of the great favorites for the pilgrims, who would travel thousands of miles through the Urals to visit the earliest of Christian centers.

Rasputin spent more and more time at his prayers. Hours would pass with him kneeling on the hard floor of the modest underground chapel where he had placed ikons, brought back from his travels, in the scooped out alcoves in the walls. Sometimes he would rock forward knocking his forehead on the ground until the skin became red and raw, sometimes he would fast.

Much as he loved his family, much as he would always feel spiritually attached to his home and his village, Rasputin's need to wander would return with the spring. He needed still to find out the precise role that God had marked out for him. In his wanderings, in his visits to the monasteries and holy places, his restlessness was given an outlet and his sensation-seeking and spiritual hunger were a little assuaged.

A favorite pilgrimage was to the holy city of Kiev, visiting Kazan on the way. Both cities involved journeying through the Urals, but where Kazan was about 600 miles from Pokrovskoe, Kiev was more than 1000 miles to the west. It is an earliest center of Christianity, and attracted a continual stream of pilgrims. A focus of spiritual interest was the Monastery of the Caves, built in the 11th century, with its vast crypt which housed the remains of 100 of only 385 canonized saints of the Russian Orthodox religion.

In his many visits to the place, Rasputin was never to lose his response to its simplicity and how purifying this could be. He wrote, "Here there is neither gold nor silver; the very silence seems to breathe, and the saints repose in simplicity without any silver shrines but in plain oak coffins. One realizes one's own worthlessness, the soul is oppressed, and one is filled with a great sadness. And perforce one meditates on the vanity of life."

Rasputin would stay a few months, mixing with the pilgrims and the monks, praying, discussing theological matters, hearing who were the new Holy Men, who were the men of influence. At any religious shrine there were always the sick and crippled in hope of some miraculous cure. There are stories that Rasputin, who had a genuine gift for calming and consoling even the most desperate and distressed, here had success in curing the apparently incurable. It would seem that at one point he told a crippled man that he could get up and walk and much to the amazement of the watching crowd, the man did just that.

Rasputin was fast becoming known outside the circle of peasants and local Siberian monks where he had initially made his presence felt. Kiev, and then Kazan, contained influential churchmen and men and women of the aristocracy, the class of privileged Russians that he had not met until then.

Kazan, on the mighty River Volga more than a mile wide, was a city founded by the Tartars in the early 15th century. The Tartars had by then become moslems and had build a number of mosques in this captured city. But they only had about a hundred years of occupation before Ivan the

Kazan the Beautiful – a place that occupied Rasputin's greatest and most happy times.

Terrible drove the Tartars from Kazan in one of his bloody campaigns. 30,000 Tartars still remained, however, and brought an exotic influence to bear on the city.

The buildings were brilliantly colored. There were houses with ocher walls and emerald-green roofs; every color of the rainbow, and every shade in between, were employed by the inhabitants of houses and shops to brighten up the doors, the windows, the roofs of this prosperous river port. The markets, too, were a visual feast for this peasant from the harsher steppe-lands to the east, for Rasputin loved bright colors and new sensations;

*The outrageous
and provocative
Black Virgin,
Rasputin's
goddess.*

on feast days the known for their their women in and multi-colored Siberians were gaily-colored shirts, brilliant blouses skirts. In the markets of Kazan, bright leather oriental slippers, shimmering cloths of gold and silver, boots and belts and elaborately decorated saddles, all assailed his senses. And then the vegetables and fruit from the fertile plains, and imported from the warmer climates to the south, these were never to be seen in the small towns around Pokrovskoe. The people also were an exciting mixture of races and customs; Chinese, negroes, Tartars, Russians from every corner of the country, Turks, Arabs, gentlemen, holy men, peasants and rogues. Rasputin was in his element and was to return here time and again.

The attractions of Kazan were not merely sensual and material. The Bogoroditski Convent, built in 1579 to house the miracle-working ikon of the Black Virgin of Kazan, was a place of personal pilgrimage for Rasputin. This ikon had been found buried in the earth and as its power to help people who prayed to it became renowned, the convent was built at the place it had been found. So precious was this ikon that it had been moved to Moscow soon after the convent was built, and then taken for safe-keeping to Peter the Great's new capital city, St. Petersburg. But representations of it remained and Rasputin liked to remind himself of the extraordinary vision which had summoned him to a life beyond Siberia, in the service of God.

Reputation... & Vilification

Rasputin's reputation, by the end of the 1890's, had spread by word of mouth as far as the religious centers of Kiev and Kazan. He was hailed as a peasant holy man, a *starets*, who could interpret the scriptures in a convincing way, and who healed people and could foretell the future.

To the Orthodox Church, saints and holy men had always added a vivifying element to the theoretical, doctrinal, bones of the religion. The schism with the "Old Believers" had weakened the reformed Church, which was aware of its need to keep Orthodox religion emotionally satisfying to a far-flung and multifarious flock. This could only be done, it was argued, by ensuring that their religion remained simple, unworldly and easily accessible. To have its spirit swamped by bureaucracy and administered by mercenary or lazy priests would herald the end of Orthodoxy and the beginning of chaos – or revolution.

So it was that the Orthodox churchmen at the turn of the century, when Rasputin was beginning to come to their notice, were eager and willing to meet and promote any new holy man, or healer, who may come their way, and thus bring a possibility of greater unity, popularity and fervor.

Rasputin soon became the interest of the society woman – perhaps no different behind the exterior to those peasant women he had so long been familiar with.

Of the influential churchmen whom Rasputin was to meet in Kazan, two were of particular note. Chrisanthos was a preacher who inspired a large and popular following. A simple man, he recognized a similar directness in Rasputin and was to become a great admirer of this new peasant holy man, a man who, like him, could speak directly and movingly to the people.

More importantly, Rasputin also met the Bishop of Kazan, Bishop Andrey. Here was a more difficult man to convince. Bishop Andrey was a highly intelligent and sophisticated man. His background was noble, rather than peasant, and he was less impressed by the attraction of personality, the simple, ill-educated manner, nor the appeals to emotion and personal experience which characterized much of Rasputin's success with the people.

The Bishop was impressed at first by an undoubted sincerity and conviction evident in Rasputin, but within a year he began to have serious doubts about the extent of Rasputin's holiness. His stirrings of doubt were set in motion, most likely, by Rasputin's increasing success in society circles in Kazan. Suddenly this Siberian peasant with his unkempt hair and beard and his bedraggled clothes, was being sought after by the smartest families in the city. For the first time in Rasputin's life he was meeting people with secular power and influence, people who – particularly the women – would find themselves fascinated by this charismatic man with the mesmerizing eyes and manner, unlike any of the men they knew.

By the time
Rasputin
entered high
society he had
reached past the
stage of interest
in all that it
represented,
except perhaps
one aspect – the
step up onto the
world stage.

*Rasputin had a distinct sexual
presence which emasculated the refined,
etiolated, drawing-room dandies who
hitherto had titillated the bored wives of rich men.*

*It may even be
that those
so-called
sophisticated
people, who
would now be
subject to
Rasputin's
power, were still
more gullible
than those he
left behind.*

This was to be one of the turning points in Rasputin's life. No longer would he belong only to the bedraggled band of itinerant holy men, wandering from monastery to monastery across the length and breadth of Russia. No longer would rumor of his powers be passed just amongst the peasants and poor monks of rural Russia. No more would the extent of his power and influence extend no further than the congregation assembled for that one particular meeting, that one particular moment. Perhaps his spasmodic ability to foretell the future meant that Rasputin knew that this was his first step onto the world stage.

Certainly no one else can have known what was in store for that arresting and improbable figure of a man, who sat quietly amid the satin upholstery, the chandeliers, the Persian carpets and finest porcelain of a typical aristocratic drawing-room – and felt at home. It was to be Rasputin's strength always that he was utterly himself, regardless of the circumstances he found himself in, or the unfamiliarity of his surroundings. He was a peasant who, although not poverty-stricken by the standards of his class, nevertheless had lived in a slow-moving, narrow, poor and suspicious culture which had made few concessions to progress in the outside world.

Although he was to make his entry into Russian society at the turn of the 20th century, Rasputin had lived all his life in a class and culture that belonged more readily to the previous two centuries. He was quite unused to any of the modern comforts of electric light, heating, other than by fires, running water, upholstered furniture, gramophones, telephones, or radio.

84

Religion was the one force in Russian society which could cross the boundaries and fleetingly unite the social classes. Kazan was a provincial city and new diversions and personalities were sought by the classes who had leisure to entertain and a desire for novelty.

Noble and well-off families were always prepared to open their doors to a priest, to give religion a certain place in their lives, so there was an inherent interest in a peasant, a holy man of the people, whose reputation as an inspired teacher and healer traveled before him. There was a vogue too in the more sophisticated circles of St. Petersburg society, especially amongst the women, for fortune-telling, table rapping and general "mystical" activities. All this, combined with the natural sexual magnetism of the man, explained why Rasputin was embraced in certain fashionable circles – and treated with suspicion, envy and fear in others.

Back home in Pokrovskoe, Rasputin's family awaited him, never certain when he might just appear at their door, almost unrecognizable he was so dusty and travel-worn. By the beginning of the new century, Grigori and Prascovie Rasputin had three children, Dmitri born in 1895, Maria in 1898, and a baby daughter Varya, born in 1900. Maria described her first clear memory of her father. Playing in the street with her elder brother Dmitri, she looked up to see a stranger walking towards her, carrying a bundle and seeming to walk with effort.

> *"He was a tall man with a long brown beard and eyes a little strange, but very gentle, set in a tired face. He looked like one of those pilgrims or singers who often used to arrive at nightfall in Pokrovskoe and spend the night with peasants, who would readily offer them hospitality."*

The family of Rasputin seem to deny the damning report that he had a reputation for abusing children – more likely one of those rumors that followed him during and after his life.

One particularly nasty rumor was that Rasputin seduced children into his evil practices using a whip, hidden in his loose peasant shirt to flagellate the innocent and corrupt them to his will. This was almost backed up in a bizarre incident which reached police records. In September 1900, Lisavera Nikolaievna Bul, an occasional veil dancer with traveling circuses, walked into the police station at Tobolsk and accused Grigori Rasputin of trying to murder her. She said that she had been walking along the road from Fagast to Kazan when she had seen Rasputin in a field, sexually abusing two young girls. When she shouted at him to leave them alone, and then ran up to take them to safety, the man allegedly attacked her and would have killed her had she not run away and hidden until nightfall.

It was a damning accusation but there were discrepancies in the story which the police tried to clarify. According to her evidence, the date of the incident was 2 days prior to her registering her complaint, and yet the distance from that field near Kazan, to the police station in Tobolsk was more than 600 miles. How could she have traveled so far in so short a time? And why travel so far to Tobolsk, when she could have walked the forty miles or so to the police in Kazan?

Despite this, the police took the complaint seriously and attempted to interrogate Rasputin, but he was on one of his pilgrimages and could not be found. Neither could they find any young girls whose family had reported their being ill-treated or frightened by any strange man. When at last Rasputin turned up and was available for questioning, Lisavera could not be found. Perhaps she was busy with her veil dance in a circus on the other side of Russia. No charges were pressed.

1900

And so it was a measure of Rasputin's confidence and strength of character that he could go into these grand houses, to take tea with these perfumed, fashionably-dressed ladies and their sometimes less welcoming men, and be able to talk as unselfconsciously about his beliefs and his adventures, as if he was describing them to his children back in Pokrovskoe.

Rasputin realized that with his increased reputation came increased vilification. The local priest had never overcome his animosity towards this man who had usurped his spiritual authority, and whose fame far outstripped his own. There were rumors inevitably about his sexual conquests, his reputed dishonesty in using his religion as a cloak for his own licentious desires. There were renewed whispers about the *Khlysty* and their debauches, presided over, it was claimed, by Rasputin in diabolic form. The more scandalous the gossip, the more rapidly it traveled, embellished, no doubt, along the way.

In 1900, the first year of the twentieth century, Rasputin was twenty-nine years old and standing on the brink of fame and influence, hatred and danger too – far exceeding any but a seer's expectations.

The Palace Connection

Rasputin first came to the notice of a member of the Romanov inner circle when the Grand Duchess Militsa caught sight of him sawing wood in a Kiev courtyard. When she enquired who this man might be, she was told he was a Siberian holy man who had a reputation for prophecy and healing. She demanded that he be brought to her.

Legend has it that this peremptory request for his presence, from a member of the Russian royal family, did not impress Rasputin in the least. When he had finished his job, he would come, he said in an offhand way. The meeting that followed showed Rasputin in an equally plain-speaking mood; when the Grand Duchess asked him about the miracles he had performed, he, apparently, denied they had anything to do with him, being an expression of God's will. But this Society woman must have recognized something about Rasputin that impressed her, for she persevered and then eventually extended an invitation to St. Petersburg, which Rasputin was slow to follow up.

The Grand Duchess Militsa was an influential, manipulative, and possibly dangerous woman. She and her sister Anastasia had both married Grand Dukes, the brothers Peter and Nicholas Nicholaievitch, both cousins of the Tsar. Militsa and Anastasia were Montenegrin princesses (their father was King Nikita of Montenegro, now a part of Jugoslavia). They exercised great influence at Court solely through their closeness to the Tsaritsa, who in turn had ultimate influence on her husband, the Tsar. Part of the attraction of the

The most notable charlatan that the Grand Duchess introduced to the Tsar and Tsaritsa was a man called Dr. Philippe who had built up a considerable practice as a hypnotist. At the time the Tsaritsa was introduced to him she had had three daughters and was desperate to give birth to a son and heir. His assurances to the Tsaritsa were so compelling, that before long the poor woman did in fact appear to be pregnant, and she was told by Dr. Philippe that the resultant baby would most surely be the longed-for son and heir. Only when the real doctors were allowed to examine the Tsaritsa was it discovered that there was no baby and that the pregnancy was a phantom one.

In order to avoid further scandal Dr. Philippe was paid off handsomely and bundled out of St. Petersburg. Undeterred, Militsa continued to parade bogus prophets before her friend, whom the Tsaritsa again plied with questions about when she might expect to give birth to the heir. This explained something of the emotion conjured up by the whole subject of the Tsaritsa's desperate longing for a son.

Grand Duchess Militsa to the Tsaritsa, who was the source of her real power, was their shared interest in spiritualism, in seances, and fortune-telling, and quasi-religious experience. The sophisticated palates of St. Petersburg Society had become jaded and decadent. The dry orthodoxies of their Church held little real excitement for the pleasure and sensation seekers, amongst the bored rich of that sumptuous city. The Grand Duchess Militsa would amuse herself and her fellow courtiers, and gain some kudos for herself, by introducing clairvoyants, healers and holy men into her tea-time gatherings. Most of them turned out to be charlatans, but they caused a diversion while they lasted. Perhaps in Rasputin, she recognized an unusual power and hoped that, by promoting him, she might safeguard her own position. At any rate, Militsa was not to be put off by his lack of ingratiating charm and was to seek him out when she heard that at last he had come to St. Petersburg.

The Grand Duchess Militsa, an influential, manipulative and perhaps dangerous woman.

It was not until the Spring of 1903 that Rasputin bade farewell to his wife and three children, the youngest of whom was only three, and set off finally for St. Petersburg. As always it would be a slow and disrupted journey as he visited monasteries and friends along the way. He walked westwards on his familiar path through the Ural Mountains on his way once more to Kazan. Here he tarried a while and then walked on due west towards Nijni-Novgorod (renamed Gorky), some 200 miles distant. Here the attractive old city had grown up at the confluence of two great rivers, the Volga and the Oka. It was summer by the time that Rasputin arrived, hot and dusty from his travels.

There he heard that the Tsar had decided to canonize a monk named Seraphim at a small town, Sarov, not too far from Nijni-Novgorod. Seraphim had died 80 years before but was still talked of with awe and affection for the many miracles he had performed during his long life. Like the hermit starets Makari, who had meant so much to Rasputin in his search for his own way to God, Seraphim had lived alone in a forest, meditating, praying, and helping the poor people – and even the Tsar Alexander I – who sought out his wise counsel.

Rasputin's reputation and position within the Russian Royal family was secured from the outset by his prediction of the birth of Tsarevitch Alexis. During the canonization of Saint Seraphim, a religious device to secure the Tsar of a son, Rasputin put his predictive seal on the royal hope.

Rasputin decided that this religious ceremony would be worth the detour. The canonization of a saint was not a commonplace thing and this time it was rumored that the Tsar Nicholas II had ordered Seraphim's canonization in a desperate hope that it might secure for him a son and heir to his throne.

Rasputin walked to the town, along with hundreds of other pilgrims. Bedraggled, tired and dirty, he joined the packed congregation. Then he prostrated himself before the silver shrine containing Seraphim's remains, and seemed to the watching congregation to have gone into a trance. Rousing himself at last, he prophesied to the assembled crowd that a new miracle would take place. Before a year had elapsed, he cried, a son and heir would be born to the Tsar and Tsaritsa. There was a stir and some discussion of the strange *starets* who had prophesied such a thing, then everyone dispersed to the four corners of Imperial Russia. But they were all to remember those words eleven and a half months later. On August 12, 1904, a son was born to his overjoyed parents.

This boy, the Tsarevitch Alexis, was to be Rasputin's passport to fame and power, and ultimate destruction. To his family's heartbreak, however, and with what would be Rasputin's key to the throne, this son and heir was found to be suffering from hereditary hemophilia.

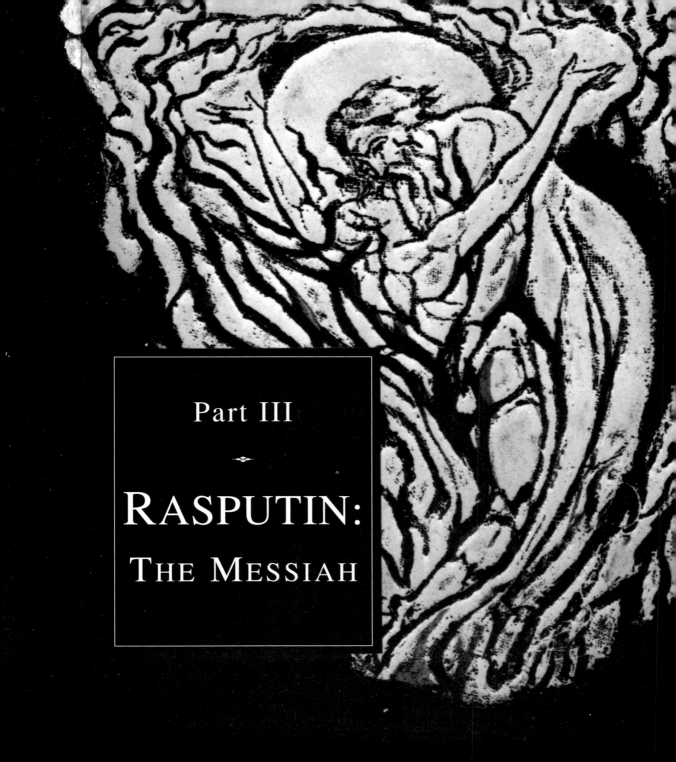

Part III

RASPUTIN:
THE MESSIAH

St. Petersburg

For centuries Moscow was the capital, the Holy City of Russia. It was the social center, the religious, administrative and commercial center of a land so immense, that as night was beginning to fall on the western territories, the new day was already dawning on the Pacific coast. In Moscow, Ivan the Terrible decided in 1547 that he was not content with being merely Grand Prince of Moscow. He decreed that he would be crowned Tsar of all Russia. It took a later and equally powerful Tsar to wrest this pre-eminence from Moscow and establish a new capital in a distant corner of the empire.

When Peter the Great came to the throne in 1689 he determined to Europeanize Russia, to try and break the predominance of the Slav inheritance, by turning Russian eyes to the West and away from the East. One of his boldest enterprises was to built St. Petersburg. He went north and even further west from Moscow and where he could go no further, where the marshlands of the River Neva met the sea water of the Gulf of Finland, the Tsar Peter built his artificial capital city.

It was a terrific undertaking. More than 200,000 peasant laborers died in its construction, wiped out by disease, malnutrition and ill-treatment.

True to his insistence on European style and spirit, Peter the Great brought in Italian architects to execute the grandest designs for palaces, public buildings and churches. Millions of tons of pink and yellow granite of the finest lustre were hauled across the vast plains to construct this fantastic city.

The enormous Kazan Cathedral, built in veneration of The Virgin of Kazan, was modelled on St. Peter's Basilica in Rome. Even the more modest merchants' houses were touched with southern charm with their stucco fronts painted in brilliant colors of pink, yellow and blue. It was a Mediterranean city, called "The Venice of the North", (or less admiringly, "Babylon of the Snows") but built in a northern climate, on the same latitude as Oslo.

94

*Venice
of the
North...*

*Babylon
of the
Snows*

Built straddling nineteen islands, with bridges and canals and the great spread of the river Neva itself, this was a city built on water. But this meant that for long months of each year the water froze as solid as crystal and great wind and snow storms would blast across the plains, unencumbered by mountains or forest, and batter the buildings and inhabitants of this elaborate Italianate city with the rawness of a Russian winter.

It was not just the architecture which was distinctively European. Manners and culture in the city also had more in common with Paris than with Moscow. Smart society came here for the most sophisticated entertainments. French was spoken, not Russian. The women dressed in gowns from Paris and were renowned for their daringly low necklines – and the quantity and quality of their diamonds, worn flamboyantly even during the day.

Their palaces were filled with the best of French pictures and furniture, their gardens laid out with the formal sumptuousness of Versailles. Corps de ballet, opera companies, symphony orchestras, theatres; all flourished and were of the highest quality and international status.

Society itself was glamorous, self-indulgent and decadent. Sex was a currency of power and entertainment, and love affairs abounded. Intrigue and scandal inflated like hot air balloons, and no one ever complained that life was dull.

The Handle Turns...

Into this sophisticated and cosmopolitan city came Rasputin in the late summer of 1903. He had been traveling. He had come via Moscow and then walked the 300 miles further to St. Petersburg. Rasputin was dirty and dusty and wearing the same rough-woven tunic and breeches that he always wore on his pilgrimages. In his hand was the same staff and a bundle of his few necessary possessions.

The sight of the city as he approached it from the south must have taken his breath away. Surrounded by water, interlaced with canals and bridges, built of glittering pink, blue and yellow granite with colonnades, cupolas and golden spires, it was a city which appeared to be more of a mirage than part of the land or the people. Rasputin was to call St. Petersburg the light of day, a light which "drives one's thoughts towards vain and worldly things" and he compared it to the light of silence in a monastery where one is shown the vanity of earthly ties.

Rasputin was said to have told his daughter Maria that although at first he was quite unaware of the general decadence of the society there, as he was yet to hear of the tensions and resentments which smoldered amongst the workers employed to service the excessive and grotesque tastes

Nikolaevski Embankment and the Church of St. Isaacs, around 1900 – St. Petersburg.

of their rich and noble employers, he nevertheless sensed the discontent and fear which lurked beneath the surface.

But on his arrival at St. Petersburg, as at any city, his first interests were religious. He sought out the impressive Alexander Nevsky Monastery, situated on the outskirts of St. Petersburg. Almost a town in itself, it was walled and moated with a cathedral of its own and more than a dozen churches and chapels in its precinct. While he was staying there, he most probably met for the first time, a most distinguished churchman who was to take him one step further in his destiny.

Father John of Kronstadt was the spiritual advisor to the Tsaritsa. He was already seventy-four years old by the time Rasputin came to his notice. He had had a lifetime of renowned service in his Church, and had been the priest at Kronstadt, just outside St. Petersburg. Father John's religious views were uncompromisingly hard-line – "medieval" his detractors called them. The absolute authority of the monarch, the immorality of liberalism and the evil influence of the Jews, were his position on just three broad topics.

Rasputin attended a service in the great Cathedral which was conducted by Father John. After the mass confession of sins, a feature of Father John's services, with much wailing and beating of breasts, John of Kronstadt had just held up the sacraments and repeated the words, "Approach in faith and in the fear of God". Suddenly he caught sight of the austere, bearded pil-

Father John o Cronstadt, wh blessed Rasputin in th midst of a church servic and then aske for his blessin in return – the recognition of new holy man

grim at the back of the congregation. He halted the service with a cry of "stop", beckoning Rasputin forward. In full view of the watching congregation he blessed this outlandish-looking man – then, to everyone's amazement, asked for his blessing in return. Immediately rumors began to circulate St. Petersburg. Father John had discovered and sought the blessing of a new Holy Man. Rasputin was also to meet the Archimandrite Theophan, head of the monastery, an old man with views as reactionary as Father John's.

This venerable churchman was reputed to have been so impressed by the clarity of Rasputin's arguments, that he asked, especially, to have this young *muzhik* introduced to him. Theophan then introduced Rasputin to one of the most popular religious figures in Russia, Bishop Hermogen of Saratov, a large town more than 1000 miles south-east of St. Petersburg. This triumvirate of influential Orthodox churchmen were increasingly disturbed by the dilution of the Church's influence by the fashion for "spiritualism" and the practices of table-rapping and clairvoyance.

Rasputin with bishop ▪mogen and ▪onk Iliodor ▪o described ▪Rasputin as ▪devil saint"

This triumvirate of influential orthodox churchmen recognized Rasputin's obvious qualities as a convinced and convincing man of God. He therefore had potential, or so they hoped, as a much-needed unifying force for the Orthodox Church, whose appeal had become lackluster in a society already vitiated by mystics, magicians and necromancers.

A more subversive religious man, of a younger generation, also made himself known to Rasputin at this time. His initial love and admiration was to turn to hatred and vilification, which led to him plotting an attempt on Rasputin's life. The man was a brilliant senior student at the Academy. He also was a peasant, but with Mongolian blood and was born with the name of Trufanov. This young novice described the powerful effect Rasputin made on him when he first saw him:

"[He was] a stocky peasant of middle height with ragged and dirty hair falling over his shoulders, tangled beard and steely blue eyes, deep set under their bushy eyebrows, which sometimes almost sank into pinpoints, and a strong body odor. He appeared as a man who had been a great sinner and was now a great penitent, drawing an extraordinary power from the experiences through which he had passed…"

Nevski Prospe[ ]
St. Petersburg[ ]
an old
photograph
showing a litt[ ]
of city life of t[ ]
time.

On becoming a monk, Trefanov changed his name to Iliodor, creating a fervent following by his passionate sermons. He railed against the moral corruption of the aristocracy, and yet supported the absolute autocracy of the Tsar. Much of his denunciation hinged on sexual matters; he was famous for visiting brothels in order to expose their moral degeneracy. There is some reason to believe that his vituperation against Rasputin in later years was based in part on the outrage of the celibate at such guilt-free license, and perhaps just an outright sexual jealousy.

The monk Iliodor described in retrospect his first meeting with Rasputin. Although biased with his subsequent hatred for the man, his memorable images give an essentially true picture of the distinctive figure Rasputin cut amongst the finery of St. Petersburg society and the more orthodox piety of the priests and monks of the Church. " 'This is Father Grigori from Siberia' remarked Theophan pointing to the peasant, who was treading with his feet on one spot as if on the point of darting off in a wild gallop...

"Grigori was dressed in a cheap, greasy, gray coat, the skirts of which bulged out in front like two leather mittens. His pockets were inflated like those of a beggar who deposits there many eatables that are given to him. His trousers, no less shabby than the coat, hung down over the coarse legs of his peasant boots evidently blacked with tar, and the seat of his trousers flapped like a torn old hammock. The hair on the saint's head was roughly combed in one direction; his beard looked like a piece of sheepskin pasted

to his face to complete its repulsive ugliness. His hands were pock marked and unclean and there was much dirt under his long and somewhat turned-in nails. His entire body emitted an indeterminate disagreeable smell.

"Grigori, having kissed me, surveyed me with his eyes, then moved his thick blue sensual lips, from which his mustache protruded like two worn out brushes, slapped me on the shoulder with one hand keeping the fingers of the other in his mouth and, addressing Theophan with a kind of ingratiating unnatural smile remarked 'He prays powerfully, very powerfully.'" Even making some allowances for Iliodor's animosity for Rasputin at the time of the memoir, the picture he draws is vivid and accurate at conveying the essential singularity of this new holy man. (It also makes it clear that his sexual magnetism must have been extraordinarily powerful for society ladies to ignore the sheepskin beard and the unwashed smell, in their keenness to fall into his bed!) Rasputin's followers were convinced of his holiness and would hear no criticism spoken against him, but the unconvinced (mainly men) were never to be sure he was not madman, fraud or fool.

His eyes filled with the rich images of the city, his head full of talk, and his heart mulling over the friends and acquaintances he had made and the revelations of character and belief which had become manifest in his crowded stay, Rasputin dusted the gold of St. Petersburg from his sandals and set off on the long and muddy path home. Not once had he attempted to pursue the invitation extended in Kiev by the Grand Duchess Militsa.

1905
...The door Opens

The death of a policeman at the hands of revolutionaries – the beginning of the Russian saga.

Rasputin returned to St. Petersburg in the summer of 1905. There was a greater sense of fear and hysteria than when he was last in the city. The disastrous Russo-Japanese War of the previous year had left a sorely depleted Russian navy and, with the loss of part of what is now North Korea, no more foothold in the Far East. This had been followed by revolutionary activity back home. The hated police chief Plehve, who had been in favor of the war in an attempt to increase the Tsar's popularity, was blown to smithereens by a revolutionary bomb in the summer of 1904.

The authorities retaliated with the same brand of wholesale brutality and state-sanctioned mayhem which had characterized Russian history through the centuries. A deputation of workers marched on the Winter Palace in St. Petersburg in order to present a petition to the Tsar. On January 22, 1905 this crowd of workers, their wives and children, stood outside the palace calling for their "Little Father", the Russian people's name for the Tsar. Without warning, troops opened fire on them and as they fled in panic, mounted Cossacks charged after them, cutting them down with swords or hacking at them with rifle butts.

Bloody Sunday

One hundred and fifty men, women and children were killed and two hundred wounded. Nijinsky, on his way to dancing school, was caught up in the fleeing crowd and knocked unconscious by a charging Cossack. Later he searched through the bodies in the morgue to help a school friend who was desperately looking for his lost sister.

Unrest spread. The crew of the battleship Potemkin mutinied and murdered its officers; peasants rose up and murdered their landowning masters; government forces executed brutal reprisals. In the end the Tsar Nicholas was forced to offer the people a kind of constitution and in the manifesto of 1905 granted everyone freedom of speech, conscience, meetings and association. It was proposed that the people could also elect their own representatives for a parliamentary assemble called the Duma. This was to quell the revolutionary spirit only for a short while.

Into this crucible of volatile passions, of suspicion and fear, came Rasputin. With his peasant manners, his uncanny religious authority, his ability to calm and heal the spirit, and sometimes, it seemed, the body too, he appeared to some to have been sent by God as a sort of savior of the situation, if not of Russia itself.

The Grand Duchess Militsa had heard of his last visit and the reputation that now surrounded him, and she was determined to seek Rasputin out when he next returned to St. Petersburg. Sure enough, when he returned at last she sent a carriage to pick him up and bring him to her and her husband's grand palace on the English Quay on the Neva.

Rasputin joined an informal family gathering with the Grand Duchess Militsa and was questioned, conversationally, about his life. She asked him about his miracles, but got little explanation beyond the gruff "The miracles are not mine". What about his prophecies? "Only God can tell me what to say"

In the silence that followed, Rasputin's eye fell on the small dog which the Grand Duke Nikolai was patting. Talk turned to this pet's declining health and their puzzlement at what was wrong. Rasputin put his hand on the dog and fell to his knees to pray. After about half an hour of intensive prayer, Rasputin rose to his feet and the dog did too, looking all together more lively and happy. "He will get better as the days pass and will live for some years." Rasputin told the Grand Duke and Duchess. The small dog did just that.

It became clear to the Montenegrin sisters, Militsa and Anastasia, that here was a man with the spiritual power (and an increasing reputation as a holy man and healer) to be of help in re-establishing their waning influence with the Tsaritsa. It had been they who had introduced the hypnotist Dr. Philippe to the royal family and had enjoyed great intimacy and favors while the French fraudster's star was on the ascendancy. Now, with Rasputin, there seemed to be another chance to curry favor with the Tsaritsa, and therefore with the Tsar.

On October 31, 1905, the two sisters and the Grand Dukes Peter and Nicholas dined with the Imperial court. The following day, Tsar Nicholas and his empress Alexandra called on the Grand Duchess Militsa, who happened to have Rasputin in her company. The Tsar's diary recalled the fateful meeting, with no premonition of how significant that one event was to turn out to be.

A few days later the Tsar received a letter from a St. Petersburg priest, who was attached as a spiritual advisor to the Montenegrins and with whom Rasputin currently was lodging. This letter asked his Royal Majesty to

"We have made the acquaintance of a man of God named Grigori from the government of Tobolsk"

…Tsar Nicholas' Diary

This recent picture of the "smaller" residence of the Tsar, Pushkin Alexander Palace, outside St. Petersburg, illustrates the astonishing lavishness of the royal lifestyle.

receive the *starets* Grigori Rasputin who had come from Siberia to present to the Tsar an ikon of St. Simon, patron saint of the monastery of Verkhotourie. The Tsar agreed to the request and Rasputin was invited to the royal family's home at the palace at Tsarskoe Selo, some fourteen miles to the south west of St. Petersburg. Here there were two Imperial palaces, situated in a vast and picturesque artificial landscape of parkland, woodland and lakes, an oasis within the most barren and hostile swampland. The smaller, more modest palace, the Alexander Palace, (it only had 100 rooms) was loved by the Imperial family and became their permanent home, more or less, for the rest of their lives. It was here, in relatively modest domesticity, that Rasputin was received and was able to present his ikon. The royal children were brought in to meet him too; the four daughters and even the fourteen-month-old Tsarevitch Alexis, the precious heir to the Tsar of all the Russias. To each child Rasputin solemnly presented miniature ikons and a piece of consecrated bread. He then stayed to tea and spent some time talking, no doubt about religious matters and perhaps about his home in Siberia.

The Romanov Dynasty

The Romanov dynasty was the result, as all dynasties are, of a marriage. In 1547, Prince Ivan IV of Moscow, a mere seventeen-year-old youth, who had just proclaimed himself Tsar of all the Russias, had decided he needed a wife. Everything Ivan was to do was grotesquely excessive, and he started the way he meant to go on. He ordered two thousand eligible maidens to line up to be inspected. From this vast assembly of variable beauty and breeding, he chose Anastasia Romanov, the daughter of a popular Muscovite family of suitable nobility. Ivan grew to love his wife, excessively perhaps, for when she died ten years later, his grief turned to rage and, it would be charitable to say, that raging grief turned to madness. On the death of Anastasia, Ivan the Terrible was born. The wholesale cruelty that characterized his reign, the refinements of his mass torturing, the unprovoked violence, the bloodlust and towering inhumanity, set him apart in the history of a country already drenched in blood.

The Tsar Ivan became paranoic. He trusted no one. Even his supporters fled the country, afraid of his unpredictable and murderous whims. He

*Tsar Ivan
the Terrible –
a painting
by Vasnetsov
in the Tretyakov
Gallery
in Moscow.
A reign of
depravity,
cruelty and
terror.*

carried an iron staff with a spear point, with which he impaled anyone who fleetingly displeased him. He divided Russia into two parts, one vast continent for him, the other for the nobles, and over his personal kingdom he established a political security force whose task was to spy on everyone who might be an enemy and destroy anyone in the least bit suspicious. This in effect authorized a large body of thugs to run amok, killing and torturing as they felt inclined. It could be argued that Ivan the Terrible was the architect of the modern police state.

His reaction to the people of the city of Novgorod, had all the ingredients of the insane barbarism and large-scale evil for which his reign has become a by-word. The year was 1570 and suddenly he got it into his head that Novgorod intended some treason against him. So Ivan marched an army to the outskirts of the city, raping and murdering on the way. Once there he ordered that a palisade be built around the whole city, thus preventing anyone from escaping, and for five weeks sat on his throne in front of the desperate city and watched while sixty thousand people were ritually tortured to death.

His son Ivan, it would appear, was equally depraved – or insane – and died at the hands of his own father. The death of Ivan the Terrible, after a thirty-seven years' reign, twenty-seven years of which were a reign of

Peter the Great was unafraid of progress and in the thirty-six years of his reign he created a viable army and navy, founded the Academy of Science, simplified the Russian alphabet and edited the first Russian newspaper. He shared, however, the ruthless, autocratic cruelty of Ivan the Terrible, capable of putting down any uprising with devastating reprisals, and suspecting his own son of plotting against him, ordering the boy to be tortured to death.

terror, had a grotesque appropriateness. Fifty-four years old, sexually incapable (it was rumored that syphilis had turned him mad) and ill, he asked a number of mystics and fortune-tellers to the Court. They forecast, apparently, that he would die on March 18th, 1584. Showing that however ill and impotent he may be, he could still live up to his name, Ivan the Terrible threatened to burn them all alive if he was still around on the day. On the 17th, he reminded the men that they were to die the next morning. They pointed out, perhaps with some anxiety, that the day was not considered to be over until midnight.

The fateful day dawned and the Tsar Ivan decided to spend it playing chess with Boris Godunov, one of courtiers. During the game, however, the Tsar's king kept falling over. Then suddenly, the Tsar himself keeled over backwards and within minutes Ivan the Terrible lay dead on the floor.

Ivan left Russia traumatized and divided. There began the Time of Troubles as it came to be called. He had murdered his son and heir and so his mentally-retarded second son Feodor ascended to the throne and ruled ineffectively until Boris Godunov seized power. There followed a series of pretenders to the throne, which further weakened and divided the country, so much so that Poland managed to invade the southern region and to occupy Moscow.

Peter the Great, an exception to the normally weak Russian Royal family, inherited the mantel in 1689, a reforming Tsar with Europe in his sights.

Peter the Great

The Polish army centered its forces in the Kremlin, put the rest of the city to the torch and prepared for a long siege. They managed to hold out for nearly two years, in the end only by eating their own dead. At last, at the end of 1612, the Poles surrendered the Kremlin and were driven out of the capital and of Russia. Having been without a Tsar for three years, it was decided to elect a new Tsar and the only choice appeared to be a sixteen-year-old boy, grand-nephew of Ivan the Terrible, Michael Romanov. Reluctant and afraid, the youth was forced to accept the terrifying office which his great-uncle had made so absolute in its power and so fearsome in the execution of that power.

The Romanovs were, on the whole, a dynasty of weaklings with some startling exceptions. Michael's grandson was the most prominent of them all. Peter the Great inherited the mantle in 1689. He was a reforming Tsar, europeanizing Russia, building St. Petersburg, but ignoring the appalling plight of the peasants. He was exceedingly tall and had enormous energy. Peter the Great was unafraid of progress and in the thirty-six years of his reign he created a viable army and navy, founded the Academy of Science, simplified the Russian alphabet and edited the first Russian newspaper.

Catherine the Great, the second of her name in Russian history.

The other startling character to emerge from the dynasty, although she was not by blood a Romanov, nor even a Russian, was Catherine the Great. Catherine started life as an obscure German princess, married at fourteen to the brutish and possibly mentally-deficient Tsar Peter III. When her husband was murdered, possibly by one of her many lovers, Catherine became Empress of Russia.

Catherine brought a fine intellect and a love of the arts to the ruthless autocracy of the Empire. She herself wrote books, including a history of Russia, sculpted and painted. She loved the great French authors and philosophers, but she too thought it necessary to subdue the peasants with fearsome authority.

Against her intentions, her son Paul inherited the throne on her death in 1796 and proved himself as much a madman as his terrible forebear, so much so that people feared he was somehow a new embodiment of Ivan the Terrible. Catherine's preferred choice was her grandson Alexander and this young man eventually murdered Paul and put himself in his place.

*Tsar Alexander III
dying, gives advice
to his son—
the future
Nicholas II*

Although the beginning of Alexander I's reign started auspiciously with talk of a constitution, it deteriorated into further burdens of cruelty and hardship for the peasants. He set up military camps in which discipline was maintained through barbaric punishments (being beaten to death by running the gauntlet down a column of soldiers, being one typical example). By his death there were over half a million peasants in such camps.

His "death" was a bizarre mystery with elements of the essential Russian character. For many years he had wanted to retire and become a monk, or go to Switzerland. When he was forty-eight he seemed to do just that. He went to the distant sea-port of Taganrog and reported that he was suffering from malaria. He refused all medical ministrations and apparently "died" four days after seeing a priest, who was never summoned again.

Ten doctors made an examination of the corpse and the royal physician drew up the report but, according to his own testimony, refused to sign it. There was little sign that the man, whose body it was, had died from malaria. The corpse was hurried into its coffin and the few who saw it said their Tsar had changed beyond all recognition. It was noticed also that his back and loins were black, blue and purplish-red.

Eleven years later a monk appeared in Siberia who was the same age and height as Alexander – and rumor had it actually *was* Alexander.

Tolstoy wrote a story about this monk in which he described how Alexander suddenly saw his chance to "disappear" when he saw a man, who looked remarkably like himself, being flogged to death by running the gauntlet (a punishment he had specifically introduced). This would explain the bruised condition of the body but not much else.

Alexander's coffin was opened in 1865 and again sixty years later when it was found to be empty. Whatever may have happened to Alexander I it is unlikely that he died of malaria in Taganrog in 1825. Only in Russia could it be possible that an absolute ruler over a vast empire should choose to abandon the ship of State in order to become an unknown, itinerant monk.

His successor was his younger brother Nicholas I. Unfortunately, this Tsar almost immediately had to face an uprising amongst his officers, which was to become known as the Decembrist Revolt. This put an end to any hopes that at last reforms might be instigated that would improve the lot of the ordinary Russian. Repression and censorship were the order of the day.

Alexander II who succeeded to the throne in 1855 was a militarist who was nevertheless willing to be a reforming Tsar. He emancipated the serfs, whose circumstances had been akin to slaves, in 1861, but although the peasants could in law now own their own land, they were prohibited from buying, by artificially inflated prices, or were yoked by debt to their masters of old.

This multiple illustration of Nicholas II shows the Russian Royal in all his various uniforms around 1900, published in "Le Petit Journal." The pictures show well the celebration of royalty in Russia, the flamboyance and richness, the bestowed power and hierarchical formality of one single group of people living a "million miles" from the peasants who would eventually bring them down.

There followed a series of desperate attempts on his life, roughly one each year, until in 1879 the revolutionaries turned to dynamite. There were two attempts to blow up the Imperial train with Alexander in it. Then a hundredweight of dynamite was stuffed into the chimney in the grand dining room in the Winter Palace, the spectacular building in St. Petersburg where the most extravagant Imperial entertainments were staged. A massive explosion ripped out a section of the palace and would have killed the Tsar too if he had not been delayed from entering the room by a late guest. Suddenly it became more than one's life was worth to be in the same vicinity as Alexander, and a panic spread through St. Petersburg society, as everyone reversed their social policy and were desperate to keep out of his company as much as possible.

Repression and secret police activity increased. But the revolutionaries were determined and on March 1, 1881 several men armed with bombs lay in wait on every possible route that the Tsar could take back to his palace. As his carriage passed, an enormous bomb was thrown which shattered the side of the Imperial carriage, a cossack and a boy bystander. The Tsar got out to see to the wounded soldier and another bomb was thrown, killing the assassin and blowing off one of the Tsar's legs, destroying the other, ripping away his stomach and a part of his face. This terribly injured man was taken back to the palace and there, surrounded by his shocked family, he died.

Tsar Nicholas II, the "king" of Russia, whose family life was so bound up with Rasputin through their child and the Russian lineage. In this sense then Rasputin became one of the most important personalities in the kingdom.

His grandson Nicholas, who was only thirteen and eventually was to become Tsar in his place, (to be remembered always for being the last Tsar of all the Russias, destroyed, along with his beloved family, by the revolutionaries' bullets) had come in from the garden, dressed in his little sailor's suit, to stand at his grandfather's bedside, witness to his grotesque and horrifying death.

Consequently, his own father, Alexander II's son, ascended to the throne determined to stamp out any signs of dissent amongst his people and with his face implacably set against reform. Alexander III was 'a man of forbidding physical presence. Enormously tall and bulky in physique, he had the brutal, simplicity of mind to match. He ruled repressively with an iron fist. But he set out to strengthen Russia externally by initiating building programs on the railways and enlarging and restructuring the army. Energetic, autocratic, unsympathetic, he was a daunting father for a sensitive, home-loving son.

Alexander III's unexpected and premature death on November 1, 1894, when he was only forty-nine, propelled his unprepared and reluctant son into history. Nicholas was only twenty-six and had had no experience of official life. Terrified, and with tears in his eyes, he fell into his brother-in-law's arms, "what am I going to do?…I am not prepared to be a Tsar. I never wanted to become one. I know nothing of the business of ruling. I have no idea of even how to talk to the ministers."

Nicholas & Alexandra

The coronation of Nicholas as Emperor of Russia, with magnificent pomp and ceremony.

The lives and all the hopes of the Tsar Nicholas and the Tsaritsa Alexandra and their children were to be bound up inextricably with Rasputin's power and life. The future of Russia, therefore, also became dependent on the influence of this one Siberian peasant. Nicholas and Alexandra's susceptibility to Rasputin's personality and spiritual power was the result of qualities in their own personalities and the peculiar tragedy of their son's chronic illness.

From the age of twenty-one, when Princess Alix, as she was called then, came to St. Petersburg on a six-week visit, Nicholas had determined to marry her. He told his parents that if he could not marry her he would not marry anyone. Princess Alix of Hesse-Darmstadt was a German princess, grand-daughter of Queen Victoria, and was only seventeen when Nicholas fell so obstinately in love with her. She was not a popular choice for the heir to all the Russias. She was German, which was a distinct disadvantage, she was shy, clumsy, badly dressed and spoke French with an appallingly unsophisticated accent. Since the death of her mother at the age of six, the little princess was brought up under the heavy influence of Queen Victoria and this rather prim, restrained girl was not to the liking of the flamboyant and excessive taste of St. Petersburg society.

Nicholas and
Alexandra
dressed in
medieval
costume for a
court ball.

It was a relationship where Alexandra (as she was to become on her conversion to Orthodoxy) cleverer than Nicholas, more whimsical, more opinionated, gained in influence over the Tsar until, people feared, it was she who ruled Russia. (Or, in the later years, she and Rasputin in some sinister conspiracy.)

She wrote many messages of endearment in his diary, some expressing a strong element of possessiveness and claustrophobia in her love: "I am yours, you are mine, of that be sure. You are locked in my heart, the little key is lost and now you must stay there for ever." This insecure, motherless, girl would be tenacious of everything she loved.

However, as Alexander III lay dying, he realized that Nicholas might be an inexperienced heir but at least he would be more stable if he was given permission to marry, even if it was to the unprepossessing Alix.

"The whole world is changed for me: nature, mankind, everything, and all seem to be good and lovable," Nicholas wrote to his mother on having his proposal accepted. It was the start of a continually devoted relationship where each looked only to the other for comfort, for counsel and for love.

The Tsar's reign began inauspiciously. During the elaborate coronation ceremony, when he was crowned with Catherine the Great's mighty crown as Emperor and Autocrat of all the Russias, he approached the most sacred part of the service and the massive chain of the Order of St. Andrew slipped off his shoulders and fell to the floor. Only those closest to him saw this happen and, superstitious and fearful, made everyone take a vow of silence because they were afraid it might be interpreted as an ill omen.

Rig
The coronati
of the new Ts
drew enormo
crowds w
people comi
from gr
distances
see the sho

In the light of the tragedy which followed the coronation, the incident of the chain falling might well have been interpreted as an ill omen. The traditional celebrationary feast for the people of Moscow was located in the open-air in a field outside the city. But this time the field chosen was a training ground for soldiers of the Moscow garrison and was corrugated with a network of ditches. Five hundred thousand men, women, and their children had gathered already by dawn, many well-inebriated by the night's festivities.

When wagons drew up with cups and beer to keep the waiting crowds happy, a rumor went out that there were not enough wagons for the size of crowd and only those who got there first would get a drink. Men began to run, people stumbled and fell into the ditches and under the relentless press of boots and bodies were unable to claw themselves up again. Adults and children together were crushed into the mud and trampled on by thousands of surging, then panicking, revelers.

By the time the police arrived and reinforcements for the token force which had been overseeing the gathering, the field looked like a battlefield with the hundreds of dead and thousands of wounded lying strewn in the mud.

Published in "Le Petit Journal" this beautiful illustration depicts a brutal and discouraging attack made by mounted police on liberals in St. Petersburg – the unrest had started but few were aware of its potential danger.

Tsar Nicholas II's reign began with blood. It continued with outbreaks of bloody repression of the increasing subterranean revolutionary fervor. It was to end in blood. His was a job that was too vast for any one man, let alone a man who shouldered it with a despairing sense of duty. Increasingly dominated by his agoraphobic wife and demoralized by the enormity of his task and the magnitude of muddle and corruption, Nicholas turned more and more to the predictable happiness of his domestic life.

As governing his huge dominion became more difficult, as his people grew increasingly ungrateful, and murderous, Nicholas centered his thoughts on the small kingdom of Tsarskoe Selo where his beloved and devoted wife protected him fiercely from any criticism and his daughters grew prettier and more affectionate with the years. The birth at last of his son and heir on August 12, 1904 was the climax of his familial bliss. In his diary he wrote "A great never-to-be-forgotten day when the mercy of God has visited us so clearly. Alix gave birth to a son at one o'clock. The child has been called Alexis." But this unalloyed happiness was not to last for long.

The Hemophilia Inheritance

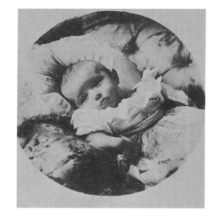

birth of the ...rtunate but ...much loved Tsarevitch ...s, heralded ...eginning of ...utin's court ...vor and his eventual downfall.

The sole reason for Rasputin's overwhelming influence on the Tsaritsa and therefore on the Tsar and the government of the whole of the Russian empire was the tragic fact of the hemophilia of their only son. It has been argued that this one rogue gene brought down the Romanovs and plunged Russia into the Revolution which changed the history of the world. Hemophilia is an inherited blood-clotting deficiency transmitted through the female line. Women carry the defective genes but rarely suffer from the disease. It is their sons, but not all their sons, who develop the disease, and their daughters, but not necessarily every daughter, who become carriers. Sufferers from the disease bleed profusely from cuts and bleed internally when bumped or bruised. It is chronic, sometimes excruciatingly painful when internal bleeding causes limbs to swell, and it tends to be fatal in the end. The Tsarevitch inherited this faulty gene from his mother who was one of the network of children and grandchildren of Queen Victoria who were either sufferers or carriers of this tragic disease. Within two generations the royal houses of Britain, Russia and Spain had been afflicted and each had their own tragedies of sons dying in babyhood or young adulthood, of mothers grieving, guilty and powerless to heal or cure.

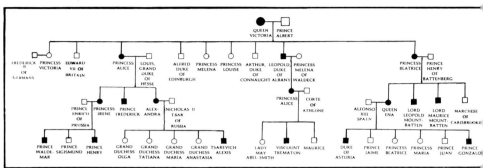

Queen Victoria in 1855

● WOMAN NOT AFFECTED	□ MAN NOT AFFECTED
○ WOMAN CARRIER	■ MAN SUFFERER

To the Tsaritsa Alexandra, the slow realization that this terrible illness had struck her son was the most devastating blow. She had at last managed to produce the longed-for heir for her adored husband and his ancient Romanov line. Her precious baby was a particularly beautiful and happy child; he was the crowning of Nicholas and Alexandra's marriage, the fruit of the Tsaritsa's hours of prayer, God's blessing on her, on her beloved husband and the people of Russia. How unbelievably cruel it seemed, therefore, that he should be blighted by this mysterious, tragic and incurable malaise. It was an agony for Alexandra to see her innocent child in pain, possibly dying, after the sort of bump all healthy children experience in their toddling and growing up.

Alexandra was already a shy, reclusive and not very healthy woman with few friends, when the Tsarevitch Alexis was born. The discovery that he had hemophilia put her under enormous mental strain and made her even more focused on herself and her family. She wanted to keep the illness a secret from all but their closest family and advisors. She watched over her baby day and night. When he was ill she neither slept nor ate. She and the Tsar employed an enormous sailor to go everywhere with the growing Tsarevitch, in an attempt to protect him from falls and childish accidents which might set off the dreaded bleeding attacks. While revolutionary ferment seethed outside the domestic confines of the Imperial family life, in her desperation to save her son, Alexandra turned increasingly to God.

The family t... of the Royal families of Europe containing t... carriers of t... dreaded hemophilia, always brou... through the female side... the male sufferer.

Enter Rasputin

Rasputin had returned to St. Petersburg in the spring of 1906. He continued to be asked to society gatherings and his reputation as holy man and healer grew. He spent as much time in the monastery and in conversation and prayer with the eminent ecclesiastics who had championed him when he had first arrived. Although Rasputin genuinely seemed to have pursued his spiritual life while in the capital, his carnal nature appeared to be as demanding and as readily expressed. He began to have a small band of disciples, mainly women, whom it is likely he persuaded that through sexuality one attained true spiritual redemption.

He was never circumspect about his sexual dealings and although the Secret Police became interested in his affairs at this time, and although the Archimandrite Theophan got to hear some of the rumors of the bizarre behavior of this most unusual man of God, it took four more years until he withdrew his spiritual imprimatur from Rasputin.

In the meantime Rasputin's female followers had taken this greasy, smelly, unkempt peasant in hand and civilized a few of his superficial characteristics. He was introduced to washing, as opposed to the

*An extraordinary
and beautiful picture
of the Winter Palace
in St. Petersburg,
1906.*

social outings to the bathhouse where the main purpose would be to sit and steam. His nails were no longer black with dirt and his hair and beard, although still bedraggled was a little cleaner and perfumed with pomades.

Although, Rasputin was never to give up his traditional peasant costume of baggy trousers and shirt, he condescended to wear the silk shirts his adoring ladies embroidered for him. But they never managed to reform his distinctively messy table manners; all his life he continued to eat with his fingers, offering stew or soup from his own bowl – and with his own hands – to his guests. And his social manner remained unpretentious and warmly primitive throughout, regardless of the company in which he might find himself.

The call from the palace for his healing and spiritual skills was not to come until the next year, but when it did the effects were dramatic. His daughter Maria related the story of how it happened, as told to her by the Grand Duchess Anastasia and her father, Rasputin.

The Tsarevitch Alexis was a high-spirited child who liked to run and play like all children. However when he was three he fell and was instantly disabled by pain in his leg. The internal hemorrhaging had begun. He was carried to his

Rasputin's great love to be – Alexandra, in a formal, though very human portrait, emphasizing her great beauty and femininity.

"he is more than a holy man;
he is also a healer, one of the
greatest of all time."

bed but the royal doctors could do nothing to stop the grotesque swelling of his limb. The doctors were as frightened as was his distraught mother.

The Tsaritsa never left his bedside, watching over him for three agonized days as her adored baby lay perspiring and in great pain. At the palace and all through the city special church services were held and everyone prayed for the recovery of the Romanov heir, little Alexis.

When she heard of the desperate plight of the royal family, the Grand Duchess Anastasia went to the palace and begged to have a brief audience with the distracted Alexandra. She suggested that the Empress should ask for Grigori Rasputin's help, "he is more than a holy man; he is also a healer, one of the greatest of all time" the Grand Duchess reportedly told her. Alexandra would try anything to ease her son's suffering, and believing fervently in God and in his power to effect miracles she authorized the Grand Duchess to find Rasputin and bring him to the sick-room.

The story of the Grand Duchess's hell-for-leather return to her own palace and dispatch of her retainers in all directions to find Rasputin was apparently one of her favorite stories.

Another favorite story is that Rasputin loved to dance and drink with the gypsies at the encampment of Novaya Derevnya, on the banks of the river, and that on that fateful day one of the messengers found him there, in the middle of a frenzied dance. When he was first summoned, Rasputin drunkenly told the messenger to be off and called for more music. Then when he realized that he was being called to the palace, that a member of the royal family was in trouble, a change apparently came over him. His piercing eyes became focused on some distant thing and he fell to his knees and

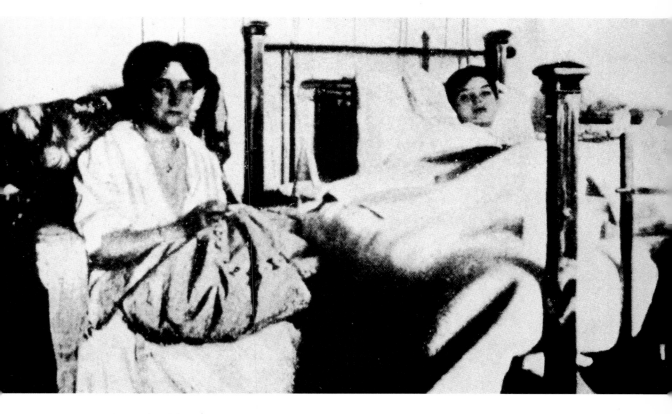

prayed. A shudder went through the crowd of reveling gypsies as they recognized the power which this extraordinary man was summoning up.

However Rasputin was discovered, he was found and brought back to the royal palace. Taken through a back entrance he walked straight through to the sickroom. All eyes were turned to him. According to the story he told his daughter, Rasputin first of all blessed the room and everyone in it (including the Archimandrite Theophan) and then strode over to the desperate Nicholas and Alexandra whom he greeted with the traditional bear hug and triple kiss. The Tsar and Tsaritsa were never to be offended by the familiarity of his treatment of them or their family.

Alexandra at the bedside of the Tsarevitch during one of his bouts of hemophilia before Rasputin became involved in the survival of the boy's life.

129

"Open your eyes my son!"

Rasputin then turned to the little boy who was lying pale and exhausted with suffering, surrounded by family, doctors and men of God. Rasputin knelt by his bed and began to pray. Such was the intensity of the moment that everyone fell to their knees. The only sound was the sound of breathing. After about ten minutes, Rasputin rose to his feet and looked down at the small boy's face. "Open your eyes my son!" was his gentle command, and the Tsarevitch's eyelids fluttered and then opened. He looked about him with a smile.

Rasputin told his parents that it was God, not he, who had healed their son, and he prophesied that Alexis would not die of the disease. Alexandra, prostrate with relief at the transformation in her son, could only believe that Rasputin succeeded where everyone else had failed. He could stop the Tsarevitch's hemorrhaging; he alone could heal him.

There were so many unbiased contemporary accounts which supported the claim that Rasputin could arrest the Tsarevitch's bleeding that it seems likely, even plausible, that he had such powers. Russian peasant culture abounds with unorthodox forms of healing. Plants, sympathetic magic, charismatic wise women who could talk people back to health, all were part of the folk medicine of Rasputin's peasant heritage.

His own powerful character also had a noticeably soothing effect on many people who came to him troubled or distressed. Children were drawn to him and reassured. He had a natural authority and confidence which stilled fear in others. And there were his preternaturally compelling eyes which made others feel, when he chose to give them his hypnotic stare, that he could see to their souls and take or give what he chose.

Such natural hypnotic influence, although not curing the disease which made the Tsarevitch's blood fail to clot, nevertheless could calm the patient and make his blood vessels contract, his heart beat slow, his body start to heal itself. Children are particularly responsive to any sort of change or treatment and the rapid recovery of children once the crisis of fever or illness is past, is a well-known phenomenon. But to the distraught Empress Alexandra, this intervention of Rasputin's was no less than miraculous.

From that moment on, Rasputin had access to the heart of the Russian throne. As far as the Tsaritsa was concerned, he had proved beyond doubt that he was the holiest of men, for to her mind God had afflicted her family with this dread disease and only God could assuage their suffering. Rasputin had proved to be the only effective conduit for God's will. All her hours of desperate prayer, the prayers of the Archimandrite, of priests and holy men all over Russia, had not managed to effect the improvement in her child which ten minutes' prayer from this rough peasant from Siberia had achieved.

To Alexandra, and therefore to Nicholas too, God had sent this member of the mighty Russian people – their "children", the people who really loved them they believed – as his representative on earth, with the express purpose to save her son, her family and the whole of Russia. In her eyes Rasputin was close to God and could do no wrong.

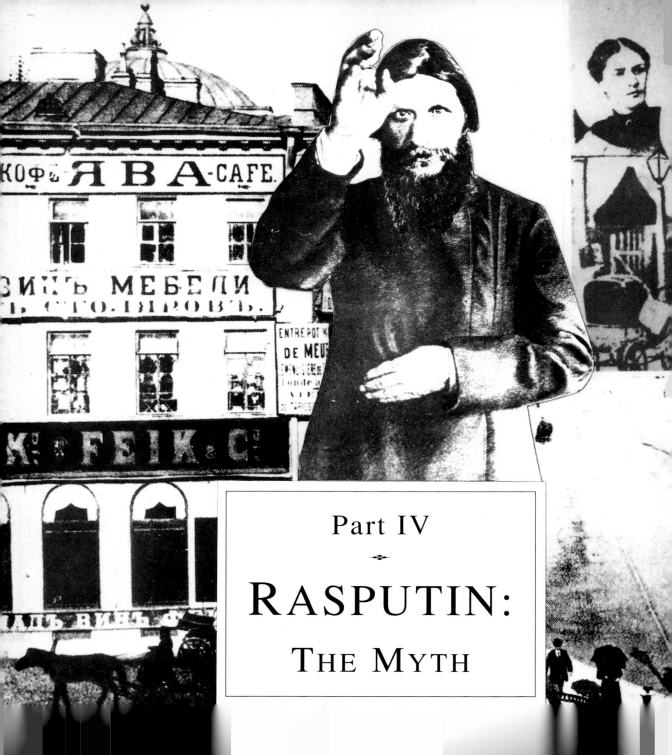

Part IV

RASPUTIN:

THE MYTH

The Royal
Rasputin

In the ten years from 1907 leading up to the Revolution, St. Petersburg was rife with rumor and intrigue. Society was bored, fearful and corrupt. Its favorite occupations were making and spending money, adultery and gossip of the most prurient kind. All interest was drawn to Rasputin. His larger-than-life character, his robust life force, his naively extravagant and unselfconscious way of conducting himself, sexually, socially and spiritually, ensured he was the most talked about man in St. Petersburg.

The royal family had withdrawn increasingly into their domestic life, largely spent at Tsarskoe Selo, and any contact with them was jealously watched and reported on. Influence with them was highly valued, desperately sought and closely guarded. They also were lonely, isolated and embattled. The confidence and reassurance this extraordinary, unsophisticated holy man from Siberia offered them was attractive enough. But Rasputin was symbolic of much more: he promised that while he lived their beloved son would not die. To the Tsaritsa at least, Rasputin was a Christ figure sent by God to save her family and their Empire.

It did not go unnoticed by the secret police or by the ecclesiastics and St. Petersburg society in general that Rasputin had become an intimate of

*Tsarevitch
Alexis, perhaps
the key
character in
Rasputin's story.*

the Tsar Nicholas, the Tsaritsa Alexandra and their children. He called the
Tsar *Batiushka*, "Little Father", and the Tsaritsa *Matushka*, "Little Mother",
which epitomized the way that the Russian peasantry traditionally looked
on their absolute ruler as the stern but good father of his people.

When he called on the Imperial family he employed these informal titles
and embraced them with the traditional and familiar three kisses. In her desperation to protect her son from pain and possible death, Alexandra, convinced by Rasputin's powers and holiness, was unquestioning in her
devotion. The Tsar was less susceptible, but nevertheless found talking over
problems of state with Rasputin left him calmed and more confident. He
also valued Rasputin's uncannily accurate character assessment of some of
his advisors and ministers.

Perhaps, most revealingly, as a mark of his genuineness, all the Imperial
daughters were very fond of Rasputin and looked forward to his visits.
They led very cloistered lives and his stories of his own Siberian childhood,
of Siberian folk tales and the different lives of his own children, enlivened
the predictable and safe environment in which these privileged but deprived
girls were forced to grow up. The children also missed Rasputin very
much when the time came for him to return for his yearly visit to his
home village of Pokrovskoe. They wrote affectionate and girlish letters
to him exhorting him to return to St. Petersburg and come and see them
all again.

Isolated from the excess and insanities of the outside Russian world, the Tsar's royal family group formed a close-knit unit, much loved and spoiled within their gilded cage.

The Grand Duchess Olga, the Tsar's youngest sister, recorded a meeting with Rasputin in the company of the royal children. They were all dressed in their pajamas about to go to bed.

"I felt that gentleness and warmth radiated from Rasputin. All the children seemed to like him. I still remember their laughter as little Alexis, deciding he was a rabbit, jumped up and down the room. And then quite suddenly Rasputin caught the child's hand and led him to his bedroom and we three followed. There was something like a hush as though we found ourselves in church. In Alexis' bedroom no lamps were lit; the only light came from candles burning in front of some beautiful ikons. The child stood very still by the side of that giant, whose head was bowed. I knew he was praying. It was all most impressive. I also knew that my little nephew had joined him in prayer. I really cannot describe it – but I was then conscious of the man's sincerity."

Rasputin, looking as strange and forbidding as ever, surrounded by his many female admirers.

Sincere, Rasputin certainly was, simple and trusting too. He had a straightforward desire for personal power, and a pleasure in the influence that he, an uneducated peasant, could wield, but he was not corrupt or greedy for material gain. Unfortunately, he began to be sought out and courted for the influence he could bring to bear in royal circles. And he was careless in whom he chose to help with requests to the Tsaritsa for preferment.

Along with the manipulative and self-serving, thousands of ordinary Russians also sought Rasputin out to ask for money, for help in finding work, or righting wrongs. Rasputin would do what he could, always in an unpredictable, whimsical way. He would accept handfuls of bank-notes from one rich and grateful petitioner and then be quite likely to stuff them into the hands of the next poor person who entered his rooms asking for help in feeding her family.

He would be just as idiosyncratic and unpredictable in his dealings with the young and attractive women who passed through his door. Regardless of their rank or marital status, if he found a woman petitioner attractive, he might greet her with a passionate kiss on the lips and start to fondle her and suggest she should undress. Rasputin had a variety of approaches with these women: he would use the religious justification that he wanted to "test" a woman's resolve, and his own, to see if they both could resist temptation. Or, he might argue the old philosophy of redemption through sin, which could come to his aid in reassuring his female disciples that their sexual relations with him were all part of God's plan – and their spiritual progression.

The "Nights of Rasputin" had become the talk of the whole Russian continent, though perhaps his escapades may now be seen as simply pleasure and joy in human life.

With his less equivocal female admirers, Rasputin's embrace (and his reputation) was enough to persuade them to accompany him to his room, or the bathhouse.

Inevitably, as his influence with the royal family increased, Rasputin attracted envy and hatred. This would have been the case even if Rasputin had been a celibate monk, but the fact that he had lusty appetites for drinking, dancing and women, and was optimistic enough not to disguise the fact, fueled his enemies' attack.

Even the religious leaders who had championed him, and had so wanted him to be a new Holy Man who could unite the Church with his zestful, miracle-working ministry, were beginning in 1910 to doubt the holiness of this starets. The Archimandrite Theophan was disturbed by reports in the St. Petersburg newspapers about Rasputin's influence and generally debauched behavior. But for the time being the monk Iliodor defended him.

Iliodor was a young and fanatical monk. He was a brilliant orator and radical in his criticisms of the Church and the State. Rasputin liked the monk but was careful to show him always how important and influential he had become, boasting about his intimacy with the Tsar and Tsaritsa, and ribbing Iliodor about his celibacy by flaunting his own sexual exploits. The relationship had begun in mutual admiration, but through jealousy – both sexual and spiritual – Iliodor's support would turn to murderous hatred.

The turn in affairs occurred on a journey the two men took together at the end of 1909 when they set off for Iliodor's home town of Tsaritsyn (it became Stalingrad and now Volgograd) and then traveled on to Pokrovskoe, Rasputin's village. At Tsaritsyn Rasputin showed an indecent interest in the prettiest of Iliodor's supporters, openly kissing and fondling them whenever he could.

Perhaps even more damaging to the relationship between them were the cases of two women of Tsaritsyn who seemed to their relatives to have been claimed by the devil, hallucinating, convulsed and screaming obscenities. With both women, Iliodor's ministrations, prayers and the sprinkling of holy water had no effect whatsoever. But Rasputin's efforts of prayer alone seemed to secure a miraculous calming and return to normal for both young women.

139

"I can have
any woman I choose"

Rasputin's visit to Tsaritsyn was triumphantly successful and he left, with Iliodor, to travel on to Pokrovskoe garlanded with flowers and cheered by the good people of Iliodor's community. In his desire to impress Iliodor further, Rasputin spent the nine days of their journey boasting about his life at Court and his sexual prowess " I can have any woman I choose", he told the celibate young monk whose sexual nature had not been easily subdued. Iliodor became more and more doubtful about the true nature of this extraordinary Holy Man who seemed to have such spiritual authority and yet seemed unashamed in his subservience to the demands of the flesh.

Perhaps there was some anger too, as he wondered how God could have given Rasputin such powers of healing and yet not punish him for his blatant and excessive sins. This became more pronounced as Iliodor saw the way Rasputin conducted himself amongst his own people in Pokrovskoe. His female followers there treated him with the devotion and sensuality that, it was rumored, characterized the followers of the leaders of one of the *khlysty* sects. Two servant girls in Rasputin's house shocked Iliodor by attempting to get into bed with him one night. He was afraid that they were trying to convert him to the outlawed sect.

Rasputin's candor and naïve boasting did most damage in what he revealed about his influence with the Imperial family. He showed Iliodor a pile of letters written by the Tsaritsa and her daughters. Gushing, girlish, affectionate and devoted, in Iliodor's hands, copied and circulated, these letters were to do the Tsar and Rasputin great harm. One of the most notorious from the Tsaritsa read as follows:

There seemed almost to be a spiritual love-affair going on between Rasputin and the Empress Tsaritsa, here seen casually photographed having tea together.

"My beloved, unforgettable teacher, redeemer and mentor! How tiresome it is without you. My soul is quiet and I relax only when you, my teacher, are sitting beside me. I kiss your hands and lean my head on your blessed shoulders. Oh how light, how light do I feel then! I only wish one thing: to fall asleep, to fall asleep, for ever on your shoulders and in your arms. What happiness to feel your presence near me. Where are you? Where have you gone? Oh, I am so sad and my heart is longing … Come quickly, I am waiting for you and I am tormenting myself for you. I am asking for your blessing and I am kissing your blessed hands. I love you for ever –"

Yours M. [Matushka, meaning 'Little Mother']

When Iliodor finally released letters like that to an already angry and suspicious public, the sinister conspiracy that everyone feared existed between the Tsaritsa and Rasputin seemed proved beyond doubt – with the suggestion of a sordid sexual relationship to add to the outrage.

Influence & Enemies

*Nicholas II
rides through
the gate of
the Kremlin
in Moscow*

Not only were the ecclesiastics growing worried by the influence Rasputin seemed to wield in the Imperial family, and the sexual excesses too reminiscent for the Orthodox clergy, of forbidden sectarian worship, but secular men of power were deeply concerned too. Towards the end of 1910, the Prime Minister, Stolypin, a shrewd and efficient minister of the Tsar's, finally decided to speak to his Imperial Majesty about Rasputin. Nicholas listened equably and suggested Stolypin put a report together of all his grievances against Rasputin. The report was duly produced, suggesting that Rasputin was deeply involved with *Khlyst* activities and was a hypocritical debaucher and debauchee. Nicholas barely looked at the report and suggested that Stolypin might like to meet Rasputin and judge for himself the character of this man he so defamed.

Stolypin's first impression of Rasputin made interesting reading: "He ran his piercing eyes over me, mumbled mysterious and inarticulate words from the scriptures, made strange movements with his hands, and I began to feel an indescribable loathing for the vermin sitting opposite me. Still, I did realize

Of course the newspaper cartoonists had a ball with the relationship between the "mad monk" and the heads of the Russian royal family.

that the man possessed great hypnotic power, which was beginning to produce a fairly strong moral impression on me, though certainly one of repulsion."

Stolypin had the definite impression that Rasputin had been trying to hypnotize him, but he managed to resist this man's uncanny power and warned him to leave St. Petersburg. Rasputin was aware of the hostility that was building up against him but rather than go home to Pokrovskoe, where the secret police were sure to follow, he decided to return to the Holy Land.

In March 1911, Rasputin left St. Petersburg with a very real sense of relief. He felt cleansed of the shallowness and corruption of that city's society as he joined the pilgrims in their simple journey south. Aboard ship, having left Odessa on the Black Sea, he confided his meditations to a diary:

"Oh, what a calm sets in.
There is not even the sound of a bird,
and man is left to his meditations
as he walks on the deck,
perchance recalling his childhood
and the futility of the world's ways.
He compares his present calm to the vanities of the world,
and he longs to dispel the wearisome torments
brought upon him by his iniquitous fellow-men."

Anna Vyrubova, Lady-in-Waiting to the Empress Alexandra, who acted as intermediary between the Empress and Rasputin and became a real friend to him even when matters had grown beyond his control. She even took the trouble once to travel all the way to his Siberian home .

He wrote primitive scrawled notes to the Tsaritsa who was waiting impatiently for his return. When Rasputin was on Russian soil again, he did not go straight to St. Petersburg but home to his village where his family were waiting. The Tsaritsa decided to send her best friend, the pathetic and devoted young woman Anna Vyrubov (whose marriage Rasputin had rightly prophesied would be a disaster had ended unconsummated within weeks) and her friend Madame Orlov to visit Rasputin in his own territory.

The long and uncomfortable journey was undertaken by the two women in part with a sense of duty to their Tsaritsa, but also with a great deal of curiosity about the way of life of this alien and extraordinary being. Anna Vyrubov was surprised at how primitive Rasputin's house was, almost biblical in its simplicity with straw mattresses laid on unpolished wooden floors. She described Rasputin's hard-working, weather-beaten wife as an old woman but was impressed by the simplicity and the religious elements of this peasant life. Her reports to the Tsaritsa were nothing but favorable.

A photograph of the interior of Rasputin's home in Siberia, a quiet and simple place with many plants and much of nature.

While the two women were still staying in Rasputin's house, the Tsar and Tsaritsa made a state visit to Kiev together with their Prime Minister and Finance Minister. Rasputin decided to take Anna Vyrubov with him to Kiev. They arrived on September 18 in time to see the royal carriage drive by with the Tsar and Tsaritsa inside, followed by a second carriage carrying Stolypin, their Prime Minister. Suddenly Rasputin was moved to cry out "Death is after him. Death is driving behind him."

145

Rasputin became a major influence in the court and government of Russia, here seen with two important ministers. His power seems to have been enhanced by a carefree attitude displayed towards the pomp and ceremony of high politics. Basically he seemed not to care and in this casual essence he earned great respect and great fear.

*"Death is
after him.
Death is
driving behind him…"*

*The Imperial
Opera House
in Moscow
after a Gala
performance –
the scene of a
dramatic death.*

This was a further instance of Rasputin's gift of prescience which would unexpectedly come to him and startle those who were witness to it. In the Tsar's own words, Rasputin's prophecy was seen to come horribly true: "During the second interval [they were at the opera for Rimsky-Korsakov's *Tsar Saltan*] we heard two sounds, as if something had been dropped. I thought an opera glass might have been dropped on somebody's head…Directly in front of me in the stalls, Stolypin was standing; he slowly turned his face towards us and made the sign of the cross…Only then did I notice…that his right hand and uniform were blood stained. He slowly sank into his chair and began to unbutton his tunic."

With Stolypin dead, Rasputin could return unhindered to St. Petersburg. But the anti-Rasputin faction was growing apace. Iliodor, once an admirer and friend of Rasputin's, and taken more deeply into his confidence than any other, had turned violently against him. According to Rasputin, as related to his daughter, the reason for this volte face lay with a terrible fall from grace, for the troubled Iliodor.

The poor monk had been so inflamed by the discussions with Rasputin; about his sexual experiences, his arguments in favor of the expression of the desires of the flesh, his apparent freedom to combine both sexuality and spirituality, that he had fallen upon the beautiful wife of a St. Petersburg officer, Olga Loktin, whose confession he was hearing.

In hearing the confession of Madam Lotkin, who was rather neurotic, Iliodor, celibate for so long, seemed to mis-read the situation. Whatever the mitigation, it appeared that Iliodor's attentions turned into an attempted rape and the woman began to scream in horror and fear at the change in what she thought was a devout monk.

Iliodor's followers burst into the room to be confronted by a distraught woman and their disheveled leader. According to Rasputin's account, Iliodor immediately tried to shift the blame for the proceedings from his shoulders to Madame Loktin, whose character he blackened by declaring she had tried to seduce him. Iliodor's followers then decided to deal with the poor woman with the primitive peasant punishment for prostitutes. They stripped off her clothes, beat her and then tied her hands to a rope attached to a horse. The animal then was startled and set off at a gallop into the country.

Bleeding and in a state of collapse, the unfortunate woman was taken in by some farm people who had cut her free from the horse and bathed her wounds. She recovered from the physical hurts but was never to fully recover her sanity. Rasputin intended to denounce Iliodor for his treatment of Madame Loktin but Iliodor attempted to pre-empt this by denouncing Rasputin first for his own licentious behavior.

On December 29, 1911, Bishop Hermogen asked Rasputin to come and see him. There in front of Iliodor and three other witnesses, he violently denounced Rasputin. Rasputin apparently answered insolently and a scuffle broke out. When Rasputin had managed to escape he went immediately to the Tsar and told him the whole story, starting with the attempted rape of Madame Loktin.

The Tsar, in true autocratic manner, banished both Hermogen and Iliodor to distant monasteries, without any opportunity for presenting their defense. From that moment, Iliodor became an implacable, even hysterical,

Rasputin's courage may best be sampled in the way he handled the powers of the time. He was unwilling to kow-tow to authority and often faced the disfavor of the established Church as a result.

enemy of Rasputin, circulating copies of the letters from the Tsaritsa and her daughters which Rasputin had shown him in Pokrovskoe, and writing his own memoirs where he related scurrilous rumors about Rasputin and declared that the Tsaritsa was his mistress.

Rasputin may have won that round against his detractors but there was plenty more scandal-mongering and envy to fuel the anti-Rasputin faction in St. Petersburg. This particular scandal was much talked of and written about; so much so that the Tsar forbade the Press to mention Rasputin again, a censorship that only drew more attention to the importance of Rasputin to the Imperial family.

The Archimandrite Theophan, who had been uneasy about Rasputin's methods of "healing" his women disciples, had finally become convinced that Rasputin was not a man of God and was in fact positively evil. His denunciation of Rasputin to the Tsaritsa got him nowhere – except to eventual banishment to the bishopric of a district in distant Astrakhan.

The Russian Duma, denounced by Rasputin as being filled with revolutionaries.

The successor of Stolypin, as prime minister, was another powerful man who was opposed to the influence Rasputin wielded over the affairs of the country. Kokovtsov, who claimed that Rasputin had tried to hypnotize him when they first met, warned Rasputin that his presence was harmful to the Tsar and that he ought to leave the capital immediately. Rasputin's reaction showed his supreme confidence in his importance to Nicholas and Alexandra. "Very well, I'll leave" he is reported to have said, "but if I am that bad and bad for the Tsar they had better not try to get me back."

Rasputin did leave St. Petersburg for his own village of Pokrovskoe in January 1912. He was afraid that the scandals and rumor and open hostility felt towards him might destroy all the extensive influence and favor he had built during the previous six years. He sent many telegrams to the Tsar and Tsaritsa from his virtual exile in Pokrovskoe. He defended his own position by playing on the fears of the Imperial couple. He denounced the Duma as being full of revolutionaries and exhorted his Imperial "Father" and "Mother" not to listen to the gossip and slander about him. Even querying his motives, Rasputin chided, "was the devil's doing. No questions should be asked."

Rasputin had every reason to be anxious. The sense of outrage and uneasiness amongst the executive classes in St. Petersburg and further afield was very real.

But ultimately the carefree and often iconoclastic attitude of Rasputin brought too great an impact on the establishment. The fear of others for this unorthodox priest eventually brought serious problems.

A contemporary diarist, a Madame Bogdanovich, the wife of an influential general with connections in Court and official circles, recorded the general atmosphere and gossip of society life in St. Petersburg.

She confided to her diary that spring, " I have never known a more disgraceful time. It is not the Tsar but the upstart Rasputin who governs Russia, and he states openly that the Tsar needs him even more than the Tsaritsa; and then there is that letter to Rasputin in which the Tsaritsa writes that she only knows peace with her head on his shoulder … The Tsar has lost all respect and the Tsaritsa declares that it is only thanks to Rasputin's prayers that the Tsar and their son are alive and well; and this is the twentieth century!"

151

A Miracle Confirms

Rasputin remained out of official favor until the end of 1912. He spent the time in Pokrovskoe with his family and followers and his daughter Maria's account of the following drama was vivid and revealing. She was walking with her father along the river bank in October 1912 when she was startled by her father stumbling and clutching his heart. Maria was afraid that he was having a heart attack and they were a long way from help. But Rasputin assured her that the pain was not for himself; "It is the Tsarevitch. He has been stricken." Maria Rasputin was to find out that her father was referring to an accident which was yet to happen the following day.

The royal family were on holiday at their Polish estates. The Tsarevitch Alexis was riding in a carriage over the bumpy, pitted roads when a violent jolt reactivated internal bleeding from an earlier wound. A large tumor began to swell in his groin and the little boy was in tremendous pain. Not only was it painful, it was also potentially fatal, threatening peritonitis over and above the general risk of bleeding to death.

The family was distraught. Nobody could do anything for this agonized child whose screams of pain diminished, with his strength, into sobs and moans. Most terrible of all for his mother, this eight-year-old boy asked her

The miraculous recovery of the Tsarevitch from reactivated internal bleeding during the coach ride, was laid at Rasputin's door, even though he was at the time still in Siberia.

Tsarevitch Alexis in military uniform. This child made and eventually broke the reputation of Rasputin in the life of the Russian royal family.

pleadingly whether the pain would go away if he died. Alexandra knew that her beloved son was facing death. He asked to be buried in the open under a blue sky. He was given the Last Rites. The doctors, the ministers of state and his family all knew that only a miracle could save him now. In utter despair, and not bothering to seek permission from her husband or his ministers, Alexandra sent a telegram to Rasputin in Pokrovskoe, telling him that her son was dying. Maria was with Rasputin when he received the news.

*The Tsaritsa
Alexandra –
caught between
the lines.*

The family were just sitting down to their midday meal. Immediately Rasputin read the message he went to pray in front of his favorite ikon, the Black Virgin of Kazan. The whole family were silenced and motionless in their seats while Rasputin gave himself up to the most intense prayer. When he finally arose from his knees, his face was ashen and wet with sweat.

Rasputin hurried down to the post office in the village where he sent the following telegram "Have no fear. God has seen your tears and heard your prayers. Do not grieve; your son will live."

By the time the telegram arrived in the hands of the stricken family, the miracle had happened and Alexis was recovering, the tumor was dispersing and he was pronounced out of danger. There were so many independent witnesses to the miraculous recovery of the child who had had no hope, who even knew himself to be dying, that even the most skeptical, the most antagonistic to Rasputin, accepted that something extraordinary had happened as a result of Rasputin's intercession.

To the Tsaritsa Alexandra, nothing now could ever shake her faith in Rasputin's holiness. His power to safeguard her son, the heir to all the Russias, her husband, her family and therefore Russia itself, was absolute. So she bestowed on him absolute power. Rasputin's position at the heart of the Empire was assured.

The Years of Triumph

Rasputin in his carriage. The white horse was a life-long favorite of Rasputin.

With his triumphant return to St. Petersburg, Rasputin was to become the most talked-about Russian, the most hated, the most feared and the most courted for his influence with the Tsaritsa, and therefore with the Tsar. He brought his two daughters, Maria and Varya, and their housekeeper Dunia, back to his flat at 64 Gorokhovaya, an unsmart street in the western quarter of the city. It was a third-floor flat with a set of back stairs that led to a courtyard and could allow Rasputin and his guests some privacy from the continual surveillance of the secret police.

Prince Felix Yusupov, who was to visit Rasputin many times at this flat, described it. "The bedroom was small and simply furnished. In a corner close to a wall was a narrow bed with a red fox bedspread, a present from Anna Vyrubov. Near the bed was a big chest of painted wood; in the opposite corner were lamps which burned before a small ikon. Portraits of the Tsar and Tsaritsa hung on the walls along with crude engravings representing biblical scenes." In the dining room everything struck the extravagantly rich prince as being solidly middle-class, "water was boiling in the

The annex of the "restaurant Villa Rode" where Rasputin's most notorious orgies were said to take place.

samovar; on the tables were a number of plates filled with biscuits, cakes and nuts; glass bowls contained jam and fruit and other delicacies; in the center stood a great basket of flowers."

It was to this flat that people came in their thousands to ask for help of every kind from the peasant who had seemed suddenly to be the most influential man in Russia. The rich came offering wads of money in exchange for some preferment at Court, or in the armed services or the government. The poor came in desperate financial plight, ill, or oppressed and in search of some champion of their cause. Women came in their hundreds to ask for the advancement of their husbands, for money to feed their children, or for advice on how to behave.

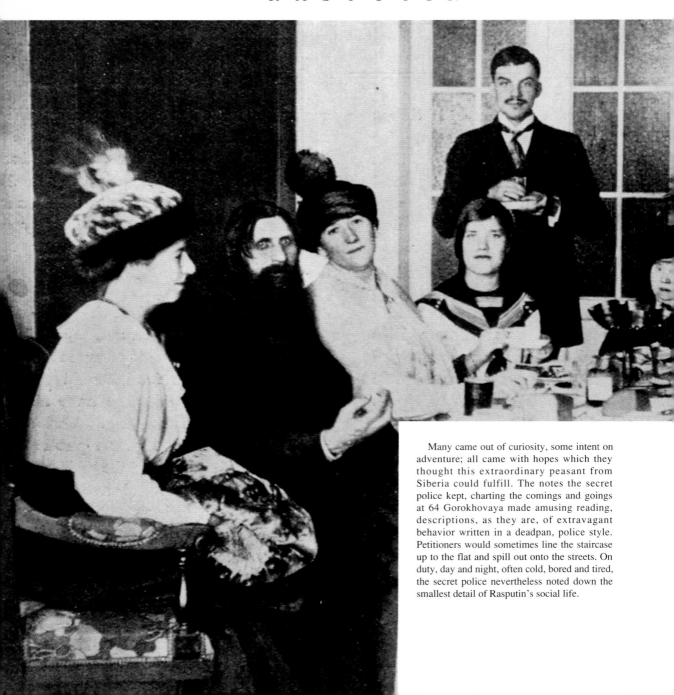

Many came out of curiosity, some intent on adventure; all came with hopes which they thought this extraordinary peasant from Siberia could fulfill. The notes the secret police kept, charting the comings and goings at 64 Gorokhovaya made amusing reading, descriptions, as they are, of extravagant behavior written in a deadpan, police style. Petitioners would sometimes line the staircase up to the flat and spill out onto the streets. On duty, day and night, often cold, bored and tired, the secret police nevertheless noted down the smallest detail of Rasputin's social life.

The Pilgrim and the Ladies

"Rasputin came home at 7 a.m. He was dead drunk... He smashed a pane of glass in the house door; apparently he had had one fall already, for his nose was swollen."

Once Rasputin had abandoned his teetotal pledge, he returned to his drinking habits with a vengeance. In the last years of his life, when perhaps the strain of the expectations of the Tsar and Tsaritsa, the suspicion and hatred of the court, the continual and increasing threat of assassination, were beginning to tell, he was often roaring drunk. Amazingly though, there were many accounts of how capable he was of recovering within minutes from the most ferocious inebriation if ever he was summoned unexpectedly to the royal palace. Alexandra and Nicholas heard countless reports of Rasputin's outrageous behavior, but were never to see him drunk once.

Reams of these police notes were piled up at headquarters and all sorts of influential people had access to them and pored over them with a mixture of prurience and outrage. Details like the following, doggedly gleaned by the detectives stationed on that notorious staircase, were pretty typical; "An

Rasputin only wrote with great difficulty and his strong Siberian accent was quite unfashionable in a society which spoke court French and English.

unknown woman visited Rasputin in order to try and prevent her husband, a lieutenant at present in hospital, from being transferred from St. Petersburg." Interviewed on the way out of the flat by these dedicated men, this lady was candid about what had transpired.

"A servant opened the door to me and showed me to a room where Rasputin, whom I had never seen before, appeared immediately. He told me at once to take off my clothes. I complied with his wish, and went with him into an adjoining room. He hardly listened to my request, but kept on touching my face and breasts and asking me to kiss him. Then he wrote a note but did not give it to me, saying that he was displeased with me and bidding me to come back next day."

Rasputin's behavior with the people who sought his help was unpredictable and sometimes whimsical, but never malicious. Certainly he had an eye for the main chance as far as his own interests were concerned, but his ambitions were simple ones. The peasant in him liked the idea that he had accumulated such an extraordinary influence over every stratum of society, his greatest power being that over the Tsaritsa herself – and by extension, the Tsar and the whole of Russia.

But Rasputin had no real greed for money. The enormous sums that came his way via his richer petitioners would just as likely be handed out by the handful to the next poor woman who came through his door. Rasputin never lost touch with his harsh, pragmatic, Siberian roots. He remained very

*"My dear
and valued friend.
Do this for me.
Grigori."*

close to his wife and his children, whom he brought for various periods of time to St. Petersburg, and he enjoyed returning to the village and the people back home in Pokrovskoe. He never aspired to fancy court clothes, grand houses, nor society airs and graces. To his death, he wrote with great difficulty and barely read. He spoke with a strong Siberian accent which made him quite difficult to understand in a sophisticated society where French was the polite language of the nobility and *arrivistes*, and where English and English culture and decoration was increasingly chic.

This barely literate, bearded and brusque peasant had strode through the rich, the famous, the high-born and the salon queens to end up at the heart of the Empire with executive power at his fingertips. All because he could ease the Tsarevitch's suffering and consequently, to the Tsaritsa Alexandra, appeared to be another Christ incarnate who could do no wrong.

The letters that people queued to receive from him, the letters for which women took off their clothes and rich men traded roubles, were scraps of paper on which were scrawled a simple message in an almost illegible hand; "My dear and valued friend. Do this for me. Grigori."

Seldom was the favor, the recipient or the benefactor specified. Many of these notes found their way to the Tsaritsa and so to the Tsar. Some of the requests, like a woman's demand to become a prima ballerina in the Kirov corps de ballet, were beyond even Rasputin's influence, but many were granted the positions and protection that they sought.

An Assassination Attempt & the Beginning of War

By 1913 the monk Iliodor was expelled from the holy order and sent under house arrest to his home village in Southern Russia. His hatred of Rasputin had reached the proportions of a mania. The personal power which had made him such a successful and popular Man of God was now channeled into a destructive fanaticism which attracted a devoted and fanatical following. His frenzied response to Rasputin seemed to be focused on his sexual activities for there was a plan for a few of Iliodor's female disciples to entice Rasputin with the offer of sex and then to castrate him. This plan failed, but a more serious attempt in 1914 almost succeeded. One of Iliodor's most fanatical female followers, Chiona Guseva, was an ex-prostitute whose beauty was disfigured by advanced syphilis. With Iliodor's blessing she set off for Pokrovskoe, considering it her sacred duty to kill Rasputin whenever and however she may. Iliodor realized that it would be obvious that he was behind the plot and so he shaved off his beard, disguised himself as a woman, and escaped to Finland, traveling on to Sweden. On June 28 Rasputin received a telegram from the Tsaritsa telling him the portentous news that the Archduke Ferdinand of Austria and his archduchess had been assassinated.

Revolution begins – Archduke Ferdinand of Austria had been assassinated, Rasputin wounded severely by Guseva, disguised as a beggar, and all hell was breaking loose in the cities.

He walked down to the village post office to send his reply and as he was returning home Guseva, disguised as a beggar, approached him with her hand out. As Rasputin fished in his pocket for some coins she drew her knife from her cloak and plunged it down into his stomach and then thrust it up as hard as she could. As she drew her hand back for a second blow, Rasputin managed to summon enough strength to hold her off until the villagers realized what was coming and rushed to his aid.

The woman was almost beaten to death by the crowd while Rasputin was dragged back to his house, bleeding copiously from his wound and trying to prevent his entrails from spilling out onto the dirt road. His horrified

"He must be stopped…
He must be stopped…"

wife and daughters examined the extent of the damage. The knife had ripped him open from his navel to his sternum, some of his intestines had been ruptured and blood was pouring out of him. They realized the very real risk of peritonitis and death from such a wound even if there was a doctor on hand to treat him immediately. But the nearest doctor was at Tyumen, a six-hour ride away.

His practical wife set about trying to staunch the bleeding by binding him in wet bandages torn from sheets, and they resigned themselves to a long and agonizing wait. According to Rasputin's daughter, all his family thought that there was little chance of his recovery.

When the doctor arrived at last he did some emergency repair work on the worst of the injury. Then he decided he had to get Rasputin to hospital. Maria and her sister accompanied their father and tried to cushion his wounded body with their own bodies as they endured the six hour journey on rutted and stony roads in the back of a springless *troika*. It demonstrated dramatically the robustness of Rasputin's constitution, and the strength of his will, that he survived at all.

In his delirium, his daughter had heard Rasputin muttering, "He must be stopped…He must be stopped…" She only realized in retrospect that what he was afraid would happen was that the war faction in the Russian government would prevail and that Russia would go to war. Rasputin himself had overcome enormous odds and was recovering in hospital during the months of July, as the advent of world war drew inexorably nearer.

"*My friend:*
Once again I repeat; a terrible storm
menaces Russia. Woe...suffering
without end. It is night. There is not
one star...a sea of tears.
And how much blood!
I find no words to tell you more.
The terror is infinite. I know that all
desire war of you, even the most
faithful. They do not see that they
rush toward the abyss. You are the
Tsar, the father of the people.
Do not let fools triumph, do not let
them throw themselves and us into
the abyss. Do not let them do this
thing...Perhaps we will conquer
Germany, but what will become of
Russia? When I think of that,
I understand that never has there
been so atrocious a martyrdom.
Russia drowned in her own blood,
suffering and infinite desolation.
*   Grigori* "

Still weak and in hospital, struggling to write, towards the end of July he sent this desperate, premonitory letter to the Tsar.

On August
1st, 1914 the
Germans declared
war on Russia. By the
end of that month the First
World War had begun. At first there
was a general euphoria, with a fervent patriotism uniting the people and
chasing away their apathy and dissatisfaction. The Tsar felt he had done pre-
cisely the right thing and Rasputin's favor with the royal family was at its
lowest ebb. Even the Tsaritsa, although never losing her faith in Rasputin,
detached herself a little from her beloved "Friend" in her determination to
remain loyal and supporting of her husband at such a difficult time.

In September
Russia's great
capital city had its
name changed from St.
Petersburg, which sounded
too Germanic for the newly
chauvinistic Russians, to Petrograd.
Flags were flying everywhere. The
Russian army was winning victories.
Rasputin was still weak and unwell when
he returned from hospital to the capital whose mood
had changed beyond recognition from the bored, decadent city he had remembered. There was no room for a fervent antagonist to the war. Rasputin would never again be truly
well, and only six weeks after a savage wounding he was enervated,
depressed and still in discomfort. Back in the renamed capital of Petrograd, Rasputin found himself ignored, friendless and,
most painful of all, no longer encouraged as the guide and advisor to the Tsar.

167

The Dark
Night of the Soul

According to his daughter Maria, Rasputin then entered a period of most profound depression. He seemed, once more, to have lost his power to pray. He feared he could no longer summon up the divine energy which illuminated his prayers and helped him to heal others. It was as if God too had deserted him. His drinking became suicidal, his womanizing even more licentious. His behavior in public became an embarrassment, to himself and the royal family. When drunk he was liable to boast about the Tsaritsa's devotion, about how "the old woman" had embroidered his blouse with her own hands, even at times descending to bawdiness about Alexandra being seen by him while she was in a state of undress.

On one such occasion, drinking heavily with a group of journalists and other hangers-on at a restaurant at Yar, his behavior was so outrageous that he was threatened with eviction. When he attempted to stand on his dignity by telling them that he was Rasputin and therefore protected from the rules that governed ordinary citizens, he was asked to prove his identity. Legend has it that he undid his flies, pulled out his penis and waved it about, as proof enough.

One of the more famous of the portraits with that seedy stringy lock of hair hanging down, giving him the look of the "mad monk".

"Anyushka, look at me; I am here."

Obviously, Rasputin identified as much with his own sexual prowess as popular culture has identified his name then and since.

His desperation was only assuaged and his health gradually restored by the ministrations of Dunia, the devoted housekeeper who had come from Pokrovskoe to look after Rasputin and his two daughters in the flat in St. Petersburg. Maria, his daughter, was obviously grateful to this woman who was nurse, mistress, mother and servant to her headstrong and demanding father.

Rasputin's life was full of strange twists of fate which rescued him from these periods of abandonment and spiritual despair. Another such opportunity for miracle-working occurred at the beginning of 1915. Anna Vyrubov, who had been the Tsaritsa's closest friend – although they had recently fallen out – and was one of the most loyal supporters of Rasputin, was traveling by train back to Petrograd from her little house at Tsarskoe Selo.

There was a heavy snow storm with visibility virtually nil and the train carrying Anna Vyrubov had ploughed into another. There were terrible injuries to the passengers and Anna herself was so badly injured that the first message from the doctors was that her position was utterly without hope. She had been hit on the head by a steel girder and had her hips and legs crushed in the debris of the mangled carriage. Unconscious and still trapped, she had been judged to be so near to death that she was left, while other victims

with a better chance of survival were cut free.

Eventually released and taken to the Tsarskoe Selo hospital, Anna Vyrubov was given the Last Rites. Although unconscious, she kept on asking that Rasputin might pray for her. Against her mother's wishes, Rasputin was eventually called for and, although ill himself, he went immediately to Tsarskoe Selo.

He entered the sickroom unannounced. There he found the Tsar and Tsaritsa, with the imperial surgeon Princess Gedroitz who had resigned herself to her patient's imminent death. Rasputin strode over to Anna's bedside and taking her hand said firmly "Anyushka, Anyushka, look at me."

At first there was no response. In a louder voice he repeated, "Anyushka, look at me; I am here."

At last she opened her eyes and spoke, "Grigori, thank God." and then lapsed into unconsciousness again. Rasputin turned and addressed Nicholas and Alexandra, "She will live, but she will always be a cripple."

Rasputin staggered from the room feeling that every last ounce of strength had drained from his body. But he was exhilarated too because, as he told Maria, he had arrived not knowing if he could cure a cut finger let alone the terribly mutilated body of this loyal friend. As he prayed, however, he felt that the love of God had once again been extended to him and he was in communication once more with the heavenly power which had accompanied him through most of his adult life.

Strike leaders arrested in St. Petersburg in 1913 - reprisals were aimed at those who formed the threat as members of the government began to fear the worst.

The Tsar in the hand of Rasputin.

Not only was Rasputin restored, in his own reckoning, to his old intimacy with God, he was restored to the heart of the royal family. The Tsaritsa believed unequivocally that he was a messenger from God and in this terrible war every piece of advice which Rasputin might offer was considered, by her, to be from that absolute authority. Utterly convinced, Alexandra strove desperately sometimes to stiffen her husband's backbone with her own conviction. In June 1915 she wrote to the Tsar:

> *"No, harken unto Our Friend. Believe him. He has your interest and Russia's at heart. It is not for nothing God sent him to us, only we must pay more attention to what He says. His words are not lightly spoken and the importance of having not only his prayers but his advice is great…I am haunted by Our friend's wish and know it will be fatal for us and for the country if not fulfilled. He means what he says when he speaks so seriously."*

And that was the tone in which she passed on these directives to her husband, who was overseeing strategy at the front. Anyone who criticized Rasputin was seen by the Tsaritsa as a force of darkness trying to obscure the light. Ministers who voiced their reservations about this extraordinary man, whose influence appeared to spread into all areas of official life, tended to find themselves without a job.

"Rasputin, the empress and the emperor;
set in ascending order of authority
and a descending order of influence."

As the war started to go disastrously for Russia, the bungling administration and lack of organization left millions of soldiers without proper arms; without defenses against nerve gas and desperate weather conditions. Without enough food or medical support, the euphoria of victory turned to anger and bitterness at the catastrophic losses of brave men and the possible humiliation of this vast Empire of All the Russias, at the hands of Germany.

Scapegoats were needed. To the angry and frustrated, no one lent themselves more obviously than the weak, good-hearted Tsar Nicholas and his silly, superstitious wife – who interfered in every matter of state, encouraged and enthralled by this sinister peasant Rasputin. Rumors, always so rife in the capital, now became exaggerated out of all proportion. The Empress and Rasputin were German spies. Rasputin's hold over her was sexual; she and her daughters were all corrupted by his lascivious designs. Less lurid, but just as worrying was the realization that The Tsar was not strong, determined or ruthless enough to control such a vast and unruly empire. The whole thing was out of control.

Sir Bernard Pares, the distinguished Russian historian, summed up the prevailing contemporary distrust; "The initiative comes from above; and there – above – we are faced with the strangest of human triangles, the complicated and abnormal relations of three persons, Rasputin, the empress and the emperor; set in ascending order of authority and a descending order of influence." To the more fanatical of these detractors, one of the ways to disable this imperial engine was to take out the battery.

Enter
the Assassin

Prince Felix Yusupov was born in 1887 to one of the most fabulously wealthy families in imperial Russia. Before the Revolution his fortune was estimated to be not much less than $500 million (at 1910 valuation) invested in land, palaces, jewels and the finest art collection in private hands. His mother was Princess Zenaide, an outstanding society beauty, who had already had three sons, but only one survived. She had longed for a daughter and when Felix was born she treated him as one, growing his hair long and putting him in frilly petticoats and dresses until he was five. He was a particularly soft-faced and beautiful child anyway and she would call out to passers-by "Look, isn't Baby pretty?" His mother's denial of his gender, he was to believe, was to be the cause of all his subsequent sexual problems.

The Prince continued as a young man to dress in women's clothing on occasions and he would enjoy attracting the admiring glances of officers and other dashing young men around town, even at one point, an unsuspecting King Edward VII of England.

Like many a young Russian nobleman, his social education was conducted in various fashionable resorts in Europe. He even went to Oxford

Prince Felix Yusupov dressed as he often was in a feminine attire to attract the court men of wealthy families. His own worth in 1910 was truly legendary, estimated at US$ 500 million!

University where he ran a chauffeur, a chef, a valet, a housekeeper and a groom to attend to his equestrian interests. He was a mannered aesthete who sought perversity to titillate his already jaded appetites. (When he was a boy, the hidden cells below the cellar of one of the Yusupov mansions were unsealed to reveal the horrific sight of rows of skeletons still hanging piteously from chains bolted into the damp walls. The house had been a hunting lodge built for Ivan the Terrible and so the insane excesses of his reign of terror were brought vividly home to the young and impressionable Felix.)

When his elder brother was killed in a duel by a wronged husband, Felix inherited the family fortune. In 1914 he decided to return to Russia, to do his duty and to get married. But by then he had already met Rasputin fleetingly.

One of the many royal family photographic portraits taken with a full line-up of dignitaries and court members. The Emperor Nicholas at center with his son, the Tsarevitch, and daughters on either side. The party also includes officers of the court regiment dressed in full regalia for such an event. The picture was, of course, taken before the revolution while such hierarchical procedures counted for so much.

Below: Rasputin's daughter Maria, who recalls countless inside stories of her father, drawn from the different periods of his lifetime that she witnessed first-hand.

Maria Rasputin was interested in what her father made of Yusupov, this notorious playboy prince and recorded Rasputin's reply. "He is a frightened boy, frightened by the world around him, by his own desires, which I doubt even he understands, frightened by the future and torn between many demons. He is a man tied between two horses, each pulling in the opposite direction." And Rasputin claimed to have recognized the beautiful side of Felix's nature, only regretting that his weakness and self-indulgence would mean the devil might well be allowed to "gobble him up for dinner." After that first meeting he had left for Oxford and a life of intensified debauchery. To Rasputin's way of thinking the devil was well on the way to gobbling him up and there was very little left of the beautiful nature which Rasputin at first had discerned.

A formal portrait of Prince Yusupov and his wife. Yusupov had begun as Rasputin's friend and admirer but once his favors to the man had been refused, the rebuffed and wealthy Prince sought revenge.

There was quite a good deal of mutual fascination between Rasputin and Prince Felix Yusupov. When the young prince swept into the room where Rasputin was waiting for him, he was dashingly-dressed, bejeweled and puffed up with pride. But, apparently, on the sight of Rasputin, Felix was overcome suddenly with the unfamiliar emotion of humility. He approached Rasputin with his head bowed. Rasputin was just as uncomfortable with this approach and so he jumped up and hugged the prince, giving him the traditional three kiss embrace with which he greeted everyone, whether high-born or low.

After his marriage to the Tsar's niece, Princess Irina, and the birth of their daughter in the Spring of 1915, Prince Felix Yusupov once more sought out Rasputin and became a regular visitor at the flat in Gorokhovaya. Both Rasputin and his daughter believed that Yusupov's cultivation of this friendship was to do with his own homosexuality. Rasputin thought he came to him for counsel and help; Maria implied that the fascination which her father held for the sensationalist Prince was bound up with perverse sexual desire. Yusupov claimed later that he sought the friend-

ship again because he had determined already that Rasputin had to be killed.

Maria mentioned a bizarre account of a naked Yusupov trying to seduce Rasputin and being violently repulsed. (Given his disgust at the practices committed on Mount Athos and his lifelong belief that homosexual love was not holy, or was not a means to redemption, as was even the most orgiastic of heterosexual activity, Rasputin did not seem a likely candidate for such a seduction.) This rejection, Maria Rasputin claims, was the event which turned Yusupov's perverse desire into an uncontrolled hatred and need for revenge. It is as likely that Yusupov's decision to murder Rasputin was fixed by two virulent attacks on the state of the Empire, and the baleful influence of Rasputin through his puppet the Tsaritsa, which were made in the Duma in November 1916. The second speech, made by the fiery orator and flamboyant right-winger Purishkevich, was violent and inflammatory and the effect was electrifying. No one had dared to speak out so unequivocally. He spoke of their defeats during the war and thundered that the enemy was within.

"this evil comes from those dark forces, from those influences which push this or that individual into position and which force up into high posts people who are not capable of filling them, from those influences headed by Grisha Rasputin...If you are loyal to your sovereign, if the glory of Russia, her power, her future, intimately and inseparably bound up with the grandeur and the splendor of the Tsar's name, are dear to you, go to Imperial Headquarters, throw yourself at the Tsar's feet, and beg permission to open his eyes to the dreadful reality, beg him to deliver Russia from Rasputin and the Rasputinites big and small..."

No one was more affected by this emotional rhetoric than the emotionally unstable Prince Felix, who trembled with excitement during the whole speech. Felix was nearly thirty and was jaded and dissatisfied with everything about his life. Suddenly his mission was clear. His search for sensation and for glory, his inflated sense of his own destiny, his desire to transcend his pampered, futile life – if only for an instant – and enter the world stage, even if he risked martyrdom in the process, would all be answered by this one bold act. Yusupov wrote to his mother the following day, "I don't know how it will all end. We seem to be living on the slopes of a volcano and the same thoughts lurk in our heads." That one thought began to obsess him and he set about putting into action his plan to save the Empire and elevate himself into mythology.

Rasputin's Premonitions

The poor warming themselves in the streets of Moscow

The winter of 1916 was one of the harshest in living memory. The great Russian army, silent in its suffering, was brought to its knees by lack of supplies, lack of food, lack of arms, lack of any concerted, inspired leadership. The men were freezing to death in their trenches. Those with any energy left began to desert. Thousands roamed the snow-bound countryside, some in half-crazed bands who terrorized villagers and stole what clothes and food they could find. The rest of the population had such shortages of basic essentials that, sometimes, without heat, food or light, the only place for many of those in cities, Maria Rasputin recalled, was huddled up in bed.

Rasputin was in despair. He was utterly depressed about the state of the Empire, the suffering of the people. He was afraid for his own life, as unrest and antagonism grew against him and the Emperor and Empress. He did not chose, however, to return to his home village of Pokrovskoe.

His conversation was full of dire premonitions. He told his younger daughter, on returning from one of his long walks, that he saw the river running red with the blood of the grand dukes. The Tsar, on setting off once

more for the front, asked as usual for Rasputin's blessing. But Rasputin answered instead, "This time it is you who should bless me" and he took the Tsar's hand and kissed it for the last time.

Rasputin also transferred a large amount of money into his daughter Maria's account and during that last month would sometimes gaze at his children and ask them how they would manage without him. When his son left Petrograd for Pokrovskoe, Rasputin said to him that if he managed to survive until Christmas then he would live on for a long time, but until he passed that date his soul was heavy with suffering.

The Petrograd Winter Palace shortly after declaration of war, with officers arriving to report for duty.

There was also an extraordinary letter full of detailed prophecy and a sense of overwhelming doom which Rasputin apparently wrote and lodged with his secretary Simanovich. Although not addressed to the Tsar, its message is directed to him and to Russia:

I write and leave behind me this letter at St. Petersburg. I feel that I shall leave life before January 1. I wish to make known to the Russian people, to Papa, to the Russian Mother and to the Children, to the land of Russia, what they must understand.

If I am killed by common assassins, and especially by my brothers the Russian peasants, you, Tsar of Russia, have nothing to fear, remain on your throne and govern, and you Russian Tsar, will have nothing to fear for your children, they will reign for hundreds of years in Russia. But if I am murdered by boyars, nobles, and if they shed my blood, their hands will remain soiled with my blood, for twenty-five years they will not wash their hands from my blood. They will leave Russia. Brothers will kill brothers, and they will kill each other and hate each other, and for twenty-five years there will be no nobles in the country. Tsar of the land of Russia, if you hear the sound of the bell which will tell you that Grigori has been killed, you must know this: if it was your relations who have wrought my death then no one of your family, that is to say, none of your children or relations will remain alive for more than two years. They will be killed by the Russian people...I shall be killed. I am no longer among the living. Pray, pray, be strong, think of your blessed family.

Grigori

According to Simanovich, this letter was taken to the Tsaritsa by him after Rasputin's death with the directive that she should not show it to the Tsar. It was later returned to Simanovich after the Tsaritsa's death.

In early December, in his deepest despair, Rasputin wrote a letter to his children too and sealed it putting it into the drawer of his desk. He told Maria that she was only to read it after he was dead. She was made nervous by his words but could not believe that his death might be imminent. She put the thought from her mind for she could not contemplate life without the towering presence of her father.

> *My Darlings,*
> *A disaster threatens us. Great misfortune is approaching. The face of Our*
> *Lady has become dark and the spirit is troubled in the calm of the night.*
> *This calm will not last. Terrible will be the anger. And where shall we flee?*
> *It is written: stay watchful for you can never know the night or the hour.*
> *The day has come for our country. There will be tears and blood. In the*
> *shadows of the suffering I can distinguish nothing. My hour will toll soon.*
> *I am not afraid but I know the hour will be bitter. God knows the path your*
> *suffering will take. You need not pray long for God to give you strength,*
> *you will all be saved.*
> *I grieve for you and for our lives. Innumerable men will perish. Numerous*
> *will be the martyrs. The earth will tremble. Famine and disease will strike*
> *men down. Some signs will appear to them. Pray for your salvation. By*
> *the grace of Our Lord and the grace of those who intercede for us, you*
> *will be consoled.*
>
> *Grigori*

In those last weeks, Rasputin did not go out to his old haunts, not even to hear the gypsy music which he loved so much. The only time he braved the streets was when he set off to see the Tsaritsa at Tsarskoe Selo. However, he still seemed to be fond of and fascinated by "the little one", as he called Felix Yusupov, and when he was invited by him to come to his Moika Palace at mid-night on 16 December, to meet at last Princess Irina, Yusupov's royal wife, he accepted.

Was he blinded by flattery, proud that this fabulously wealthy and high-born couple should seek him out? Was he genuinely curious about Princess Irina, believing that she needed his help? Or did he feel that he was following a preordained path; did Rasputin know he was going to his death?

December 16, 1916 – Rasputin predicted "I feel my end is near. They'll kill me, and then the throne won't last three months." The beginning of the end.

The Prophecy
Comes True

The taking of Moscow; unrest of the ole of Russia reaches an ›precedented climax.

December 16th, 1916 was as cold as any other day that cruel winter. Rasputin's movements, as ever, were dutifully noted down by the secret police who hung around the door and stamped and swore in the cold. Their man left for church, followed by police guards, and went on to the bathhouse, for his much enjoyed steaming. He returned mid-morning to his apartment where the day's petitioners were already assembled. There was one woman of interest, a writer and occultist, who challenged Rasputin about the damage he was doing to the Tsar and the country. His answers were humble and suppliant; he did love the Tsar, but agreed that he had been inadvertently responsible for some things that had damaged him and his family. Then he slipped once more into his premonitory state,

> *" I feel my end is near. They'll kill me, and then the throne won't last three months."*

There then followed an anonymous phone call telling him that he would be assassinated. This was not an unexpected message, it had happened

Purishkevich, a member of the Duma and one of Rasputin's assassins.

before, but it did not improve Rasputin's mood. He turned to the consolations of alcohol at lunch time and spent half the afternoon in a drunken sleep.

By the time Anna Vyrubov had arrived Rasputin had managed to sober up. She gave him a present from the Empress of an ikon signed on the back by herself and all her children. When she heard that Rasputin was to go out that night to the Yusupov palace she urged him not to go. Anna Vyrubov thought that it was an insult to be asked to go at midnight, that if the Yusupovs wanted to see him they should do it openly and not humiliate him in this way. Rasputin said he would not go.

Then Protopopov, the Minister for Interior Affairs, a friend of Rasputin's and one of the inadequate people for whom Rasputin's influence had secured powerful posts, arrived to report the day's proceedings. He told Rasputin that there was a good deal of evidence collected by the secret police and other sources which pointed to a concerted plan against his life. He was adamant that Rasputin should not go out that night. Rasputin agreed, but when Protopopov left he began to get ready to go out.

Yusupov came to Rasputin's door just after midnight. Another of the conspirators, Dr. Lazovert, was acting as his chauffeur. He had already provided the cyanide with which the cakes and wine which was to be offered to Rasputin had been laced. Back in the specially prepared basement room in the vast Moika Palace, the other three plotters waited.

*Grand Duke
Dmitri
Pavlovich, a
Russian noble,
also involved in
the murder of
Rasputin.*

The Grand Duke Dmitri Pavlovich, an elegant and dissipated young cousin of the Tsar who, rumor had it, had had a homosexual affair with Yusupov when they were younger, waited nervously in the company of Purishkevich, the member of the Duma who had made the emotional speech denouncing Rasputin, and Captain Soukhotin, an army officer.

The plan was to bring Rasputin back to this room in the palace and to have a gramophone playing in the state rooms above to give the impression that a party was in full swing at which the Princess Irina was hostess. While they waited for her to appear (she was actually in the Crimea) they hoped to induce Rasputin to eat the poisoned cakes and drink the poisoned wine. This, they were assured by Lazovert, would surely kill him. There was enough cyanide in even one cake to kill an elephant.

Rasputin appeared more carefully dressed and groomed than anyone had seen him before. He wore a silk shirt embroidered by the Tsaritsa with corn-flowers. His breeches were velvet and his highly polished boots looked brand new. His hair and beard were unusually clean and combed and smelled of cheap soap. Rasputin had made a great effort with his appearance this night; he perhaps thought he was to meet the Princess Irina – or perhaps knew he was to meet his death.

He seemed highly nervous as Felix Yusupov showed him into the room and offered him at first a biscuit. Yusupov was also highly anxious and they

started a stilted conversation. Upstairs the gramophone was playing "Yankee Doodle Dandy" and Felix explained his wife would be down soon when her guests had left. He then offered Rasputin a poisoned cake. At first this was refused and the already nervous Prince started to sweat. Then, absent-mindedly, Rasputin ate one cake, and then another.

Yusupov was fearful and fascinated. Surely the poison would begin to take its effect. Two cakes provided enough cyanide to kill half a dozen men. Yusupov gazed at the peasant opposite him who continued to make conversation and showed no sign of distress.

He turned to his next line of attack. There were two poisoned glasses. Would Rasputin like some wine? Again he refused, but changed his mind

The scene of Rasputin's murder – the Moika Palace of Yusupov, one of the wealthiest families in Russia.

when he saw Felix pour out two glasses of wine. He took a glass, an unpoisoned one, and quaffed it quickly. Then he asked for his favorite, Madeira, but protested that he wanted it in the same glass when the Prince attempted to pour it into one of the poisoned wine glasses.

Prince Yusupov was near collapse with the tension of the deed he was intent on doing, but seemed unable to effect. He engineered an accident and in the process broke Rasputin's glass which, therefore, meant that he had to accept the Madeira in the one into which a minute measure of liquid potassium cyanide had been placed.

At last it seemed that the poison began to take some toll. Rasputin drank slowly and complained of a slight irritation in his throat. He asked for

another glass of Madeira and was given a second poisoned glass. Then he saw the Prince's guitar propped in a corner and asked Felix to sing him gypsy songs, one of Yusupov's party pieces. He kept his desperate assassin playing until 2.30 in the morning, the Prince showing more signs of distress than his victim.

By now Felix Yusupov was hallucinating. He fancied that this was a duel between himself and Rasputin, between good and evil. He felt certain that Rasputin was exerting his formidable power in order to defeat him; "...confronted by those satanic eyes I was beginning to lose my self control."

Yusupov brought cyanide-dosed cakes and poisoned wine, which he was assured were strong enough to kill an elephant. He hoped to lure the powerful priest back to a room in the palace where he would offer the food and drink to him. The plan, however, took a grat deal more to fulfill.

With the excuse that he would go and see whether his wife was ready to come down and meet Rasputin, Yusupov staggered upstairs to ask advice of his co-conspirators. They were in an even more distraught state. Dr. Lazovert had fainted with the strain and was barely sensible. The young and delicate Grand Duke Dmitri wished to abandon the whole idea and the pugnacious Purishkevich thought the time had come for a joint attack.

They started to descend the staircase together when Felix, perhaps wishing to be the one responsible for the striking this historic blow, signaled them to a halt and grabbing Dmitri's revolver returned to the room alone.

Before Yusupov finally managed to shoot Rasputin in the back, the incredibly powerful and resilient peasant had drunk several glasses of cyanide-poisoned wine and poisoned cakes without apparent ill-effect. Only when pointed towards a crucifix did Rasputin realize what was happening and as he stood before it, Yusupov fired the shot.

Rasputin was slumped over the table complaining of feeling unwell. But when he drank another glass of Madeira his spirits improved and he asked Felix to accompany him to the place where he was happiest, and where he had been unable to visit for weeks through fear of assassination. He wanted his friend to go with him to the gypsies for more music, drinking and dancing.

Yusupov, emotionally highly strung at the best of times, now exhausted

and terrified, began to believe that this extraordinary stamina and resistance was a sign that Rasputin was protected by some supernatural power. And that power, he had convinced himself, was evil.

In an attempt at counteracting this protective shield, Yusupov maneuvered Rasputin over to a beautiful crucifix. Rasputin looked at it but said he preferred the inlaid chest on which it stood. Then Yusupov told him it would be better if he prayed. Perhaps Rasputin realized then what lay ahead. He began to make the sign of the cross. Yusupov felt the evil would be momentarily neutralized by this sacred symbol and then he would be able to kill his reluctant victim. He pulled the revolver out and shot him in the back.

Rasputin fell to the floor with a roar. He lay twitching on the polar bear skin which was used as a luxurious rug on the stone floor. Rasputin's blood seeped out, brilliant against the snow white fur. The conspirators had rushed down the stairs, revolvers drawn. As they made to shoot him again they noticed he had stopped twitching. After a cursory examination Dr. Lazovert pronounced him dead. Quickly they moved Rasputin off the bear skin in case his blood stained it too extensively. They switched off the light and went upstairs to discuss the next move.

But something drew Yusupov back to the body. Maria Rasputin suggests it was a perverted sexual hatred that made him wish to gloat over the

man whose sexual prowess had been legendary, but who had rejected his advances without a second thought.

Yusupov admitted he was fascinated but only recalls that he was overcome with a fit of rage and started to shake the bleeding body. Suddenly, to his absolute horror, the lifeless "corpse" shuddered into life. One eye fluttered open and, with an animal roar, Rasputin leapt to his feet and tried to strangle his attacker. Foaming at the mouth and bleeding, Rasputin kept repeating the terrified Prince's name, "Felix...Felix...Felix"

Frozen to the spot with terror, Yusupov eventually found the ability to run. He tore himself away from Rasputin's grasp, leaving his epaulet in his hand, and ran up the stairs crying out that Rasputin was still alive.

Rasputin crawled up the stairs after him, opened the door into the enormous courtyard and began running after the fleeing Prince, calling, "Felix, Felix, I'll tell the Tsaritsa". Purishkevich, revolver in hand, could barely

With an animal roar
the corpse
leapt to his feet

believe his eyes. Rasputin was deathly pale but loping quite fast away from him.

He raised his revolver and fired two shots. These missed but his third shot hit him square in the back and the fourth brought him crumbling to the ground. Purishkevich ran up and kicked Rasputin's inert body viciously in the head. Immediately a great purple wound opened up.

Yusupov then appeared, explaining he had not been running away in a panic but was only trying to cut off Rasputin's escape route. But when he heard that the corpse was lying in the landing he lost all control and flew into a frenzied attack on the multi-wounded bleeding body, beating it about the head and shoulders until he fainted and was carried away.

Maria Rasputin suggested that Yusupov's frenzy drove him to mutilate her father's body, castrating him in a perverse excitement and revenge. Indeed, her co-author in her book published in 1977, claimed to have been shown the relic of Rasputin's penis by an old white Russian lady exiled in Paris.

Whatever the truth, the much abused body of Rasputin was then tied up in a cloth shroud and put in the trunk of the car. Everyone but Yusupov, who had collapsed with the tension of the night's work, drove off to the pre-arranged point on the Petrovsky bridge. They failed to heave the body over the parapet the first time, then on their second try, the body, with blood seeping through its makeshift shroud, was dropped into the icy water.

The Palace of Yusupov seen the eerie scene of a gruesome murder, in the late afternoon light of Petrograd.

The chapel ere Nicholas, lexandra and Rasputin worshipped, and where for a short while Rasputin was buried.

The Final Battle

Maria Rasputin feared something had happened to her father when she awoke the next morning and found his bed unslept in. The police had had reports of shots fired at the Yusupov palace, there were rumors and counter-rumors. The Tsaritsa wrote a hurried and desperate letter to her husband at the front:

"We are sitting here together – can you imagine our feelings – thoughts – our Friend has disappeared. Yesterday A. [Anna Vyrubov] saw him and he said Felix asked him to come in the night, a motor would fetch him to see Irina...

"This night big scandal in Yusupov's house, big meeting. Dmitri, Purishkevich etc. all drunk. Police heard shots, Purishkevich came out screaming to the Police that our Friend was killed. Police searching and Justice entered now in Yusupov's house...

"Chief of Police has sent for Dmitri. Felix wished to leave tonight for Crimea. Begged [Protopopov] to stop him.

"Our Friend was in good spirits but nervous these days...Felix pretends he never came to the house and never asked him...I can't and won't believe he has been killed. God have mercy."

Yusupov Palace reflected in the Moika Canal where Rasputin finally succumbed to death, after multiple bullet wounds, dying only from drowning.

Then Maria was told the next day that police divers had found the body of her father. Would she come and identify him? They warned her that he had been horribly injured and it was a dreadful sight. The corpse had been placed in a shed by the bridge from which he had been thrown. His daughter entered the modest hut and was faced with evidence of the full horror of what those five men had done to her father.

Ice was melting and dripping off her father's clothes and onto the floor. His familiar face was horribly distorted by the smashed-in temple and an eye hanging against his cheek by a filament of muscle. Blood clots were matted into his hair and his wrists showed raw rope burns where he had struggled to free himself once the freezing water had revived him. It was a piteous sight to see his one free hand with its index finger raised, apparently in the process of making the sign of the cross.

There was something even more shocking in the realization that all the poison, the bullets, the beatings, had failed to kill this man. That only when

From water, to earth,
to fire
and lastly to the wind...

he was thrown, trussed and wounded into the sub-zero temperatures of the frozen river did he finally have to give up his fight for life. The autopsy found that his lungs were full of water, that it was drowning which killed Rasputin.

News spread fast that Rasputin was dead. There was rejoicing in the cities, amongst the courtiers and ministers, but the peasants, when they heard, were saddened and enraged that a simple and honest *muzhik* like themselves, who had risen to extraordinary heights of influence, had been eliminated by members of the decadent aristocracy and the corrupt politicians who conspired to protect their own interest and keep the peasants down.

Rasputin was buried on the 22nd December, in the foundations of the center aisle in a church being built by Anna Vyrubov's direction at Tsarskoe Selo. All the royal family were present as the plain coffin with Rasputin, and the ikon bearing the signatures of the Tsaritsa and her children, was lowered into the hard, cold earth.

The Tsaritsa began to cry. The Tsar committed a restrained description of the simple ceremony to his diary which revealed something of his anger and shock at the deed; "Just after eight the whole family went to the field where we were present at a sad spectacle; the coffin with the body of the unforgettable Grigori, killed on the night of the 16th by *savages* in the house of F. Yusupov, was let down into the grave."

201

"Russia is finished; They'll bury us together"

Bolsheviks
canvassing during
the early stages of
the Revolution

1917

Rasputin was not allowed to remain in that consecrated earth for long. On March 8, 1917 the Russian Revolution began in Petrograd. It started with rioting in the capital city over the bread short-ages. By the end of the month the Tsar had abdicated and by the following month Lenin had returned in triumph after ten years in exile, although he would have to wait until November to seize power.

*The Russian
Volcano
erupts*

In that cold spring of 1917, with the Royal Family already prisoners in their palace at Tsarskoe Selo, orders were given to dig up Rasputin's remains. His blackened corpse was shipped in a packing case to an undistinguished spot outside the capital and there a bonfire was made and Rasputin's body was quickly turned to ashes and scattered on the wind. Having been restored to all the elements in turn; from water, to earth, to fire and lastly to the wind, it is perhaps appropriate that the last words should be Rasputin's own, ringing with prophecy.

Top:
Stalin & Lenin speaking on a makeshift platform during 1917.

Left:
The last picture of the Imperial Family, shortly before they were massacred on the night of July 14, 1918.

*A procession
of the
"Black Band"
of revolutionaries.*

Related to a contemporary journalist and quoted by *de Jonge*, Rasputin said in the last weeks of his life:

*"The fools don't understand who I am.
A sorcerer, perhaps, a sorcerer may be.
They burn sorcerers, and so let them burn me too.
But there is one thing they do not realize.
If they do burn me, Russia is finished;
they'll bury us together."*

The Myth Endures

Russian people had more to fear from their compatriots than from their so-called enemy.

Rasputin's life and death were so extraordinary and were intimately connected with such cataclysmic political and social events that it was inevitable that his myth would live on. Exaggeration, grotesqueness, sensationalism, were the elements which added spice to an already steaming brew. An unkept, wild-eyed, lecherous man glowered from celluloid, as numerous films saw the cinematic potential of his story. First off was a German film made in 1928, directed by Martin Berger and called *Rasputin's Liebesabenteuer*, translated into "The Holy Devil".

M.G.M. brought out "Rasputin and the Empress" in 1932 as a Barrymore production with Lionel Barrymore as Rasputin and John and Ethel Barrymore playing Nicholas and Alexandra. This film proved to be a boon to the impoverished Yusupovs, who were living in exile having lost to the Revolution their legendary wealth. Princess Irina issued a libel action in 1934 against M.G.M. for implying that Rasputin had seduced her. The case was brought to the High Court in London and she had to endure five hours of ferocious cross-examination about her private life. For her pains she won $25,000, a considerable sum in those days.

There followed, in 1960, an amazingly 'sixties and sexy Italian film, called in English "Nights of Rasputin" and featuring bouffant-haired, high-heeled, Italian lovelies in various stages of undress. Christopher Lee brought all his chilling dignity to "Rasputin The Mad Monk", a Hammer Film issued in 1966, and Tom Baker played a rather sweaty, bulging-eyed Rasputin in the epic "Nicholas and Alexandra" issued by Colombia Pictures in 1971.

Books too tumbled from the presses, starting with Iliodor's own vitriolic attack, *The Holy Devil*, in which Rasputin stalked Russia as a manipulative, alcoholic, con-man of the highest order. Perhaps the most sensational and fictive of all the many books and memoirs written about Rasputin were those written by William LeQueux. Rasputin's larger-than-life qualities must have found an answering flamboyance in LeQueux, for with a cavalier disregard for the facts, he wove a lurid picture of Rasputin as monk, satyr and criminal.

The most recent full-length biography and the best, was *The Life and Times of Grigorii Rasputin* by Alex de Jonge who interpreted the contradictions of Rasputin's character and motivation with sympathy and lack of moralizing.

Rasputin seems also to have been subject to the plight of all saints and

pseudo-saints. There was at least one relic of his legendary sexual organ, castrated, it was rumored, by the sex-crazed Yusupov in that terrible prolonged assassination in 1916. Maria Rasputin's co-author of her third book, Patte Barham, was taken to visit a very old and frail lady, a white Russian, living in exile in Paris and keeping alive the memory of her "Christ". There she was shown, with due reverence, a polished wooden box lined in velvet which contained "what looked like a blackened, overripe banana, about a foot long". Not surprisingly, she was rendered speechless for a moment. Some excited questions then elicited the information that one of Yusupov's servants had recovered it from the scene of the murder and had given it to the old lady.

The ikon with which he was buried was also retrieved when Rasputin's coffin was disinterred and was eventually sold for a great deal of money to an American collector. His diamond ring, given to him by the Empress, legend has it, was cut from his finger and ended up, after various adventures, in the ownership of the poet Yevtushenko. His real legacy is a fascinating account of the true revolutionary; a man of God passionately experimenting with the gift of life. The power of the man lives on.

BIBLIOGRAPHY

De Jonge, Alex *The Life and Times of Grigorii Rasputin*, 1982
Dobson, Christopher *Prince Felix Yusupov*, 1989
Massie, Robert *Nicholas and Alexandra*, 1968
Pares, Sir Bernard *The Fall of the Russian Monarchy*, 1939
Rasputin, Maria *My Father*, 1934
Rasputin, Maria and Patte Barham *Rasputin, The Man Behind the Myth*, 1977
Szamuely, Tibor *The Russian Tradition*, 1974
Wilson, Colin *Rasputin and the Fall of the Romanovs*, 1964
Yusupov, Prince Felix *Rasputin, His Malignant Influence
 and His Assassination*, 1927
Le Petit Journal, France
Le Journal, France
Historia Magazine, Italy
Twigger Book Finding Service, England
Museum of Paris
The National Portrait Gallery of London
British Library
Victoria and Albert Museum
Tretyakov Art Gallery, Moscow

AKNOWLEDGEMENTS

John Massey Stewart: 12, 14, 24, 71, 72, 78/79, 86, 121, 132, 144, 145, 152, 188,
  196, 199, 200
Barnabys Picture Library: 63
Hulton Picture Company: 89
Mary Evans Picture Library: 20, 29, 39, 114/115, 116, 122, 163, 171, 202
National Film Archive, London: 138, 148/149, 161, 192/193
London Illustrated News: 176/177, 203
Sandipa Gould Griffin, Labyrinth Publishing: 36, 54 center, 64/65, 67, 88
Hand Colored Photographs, Sandipa Gould Griffin: cover, 2, 3, 6, 11, 15, 166/167,
  182/183, 202, 203